912   25120
Atl   J.B. Post
An Atlas of Fantasy

DATE DUE			
MAY 2 7 1987			
FEB 0 3 1988			
FEB 1 0 1988			
FEB 2 2 1989			
APR 1 8 1989			
MAR 4			
MAR 4 1992			
APR 8 1992			
NOV 2 5 1992			
OCT 2 0 1993			

Antioch Community High School

1133 S. Main Street

Antioch, Illinois 60002

An Atlas of Fantasy

Compiled by J. B. Post

BALLANTINE BOOKS • NEW YORK

To family and friends,
hostages to fortune all

Text and selection copyright © 1973, 1979 by J. B. Post

Introduction copyright © 1979 by Lester del Rey

All rights, including those of recording and translation, are reserved in the United States, Canada, United Kingdom, and under the Universal, Pan-American, and Berne Copyright Conventions. No portion of this book, except for brief quotations in connection with critical articles or reviews, may be printed or reproduced without the express, written consent of the Publishers. For information, write: The Mirage Press, Ltd., P.O. Box 7687, Baltimore, Maryland 21207 U.S.A.

Published in the United States by Ballantine Books, a division of Random House, Inc., New York, and simultaneously in Canada by Ballantine Books of Canada, Ltd., Toronto, Canada.

Library of Congress Catalog Card Number: 79-63506

ISBN 0-345-27399-0

This edition published by arrangement with The Mirage Press, Ltd.

Manufactured in the United States of America

First Ballantine Books Edition: June 1979

1 2 3 4 5 6 7 8 9

Grateful acknowledgement is made for permission to reproduce maps from the following sources:

Atlantic Ocean and the Azores from *The European Discovery of America: The Northern Voyages A.D. 500–1600* by Samuel Eliot Morison. Copyright © 1971 by Samuel Eliot Morrison. Reprinted by permission of Oxford University Press, Inc. ● Utopia from the article "Mapping Utopia" by Brian Goodey, *Geographical Review*, January 1970, Vol. 60, No. 1. Reproduced courtesy of the American Geographical Society. ● Hell © 1928 by Eugene Cox. ● Pilgrim's Progress illustration by Robert Lawson. From the book *Pilgrim's Progress* by John Bunyan, edited by Mary Godolphin. Copyright 1939 by Frederick A. Stokes Company. Copyright © renewed 1967 by John W. Boyd, Executor of Robert Lawson. Reproduced by permission of J.B. Lippincott Company. ● The Dear County, Allington, and Barchester Close © 1948 by Florence Ewing. ● A Map of the County of Barsetshire from *Jutland Cottage*, by Angela Thirkell. Copyright 1953 by Alfred A. Knopf, Inc. Reprinted by permission of Alfred A. Knopf, Inc. ● Dartmoor © 1952 by Julian Wolff. Operation Reichenbach © 1948 by Julian Wolff. Reproduced courtesy of Julian Wolff. ● Chairman Island from *A Long Vacation* by Jules Verne. Copyright © 1967 by Holt, Rinehart & Winston. Reprinted by permission of Holt, Rinehart & Winston. ● Oz maps copyright © 1979 by James E. Haff and Dick Martin. Reproduced by permission of the International Wizard of Oz Club, Inc. ● Edgar Rice Burroughs maps reproduced with the permission of Edgar Rice Burroughs, Inc. See map pages for individual copyright notices. ● Pooh's Turf from *Winnie-the-Pooh* by A.A. Milne. Copyright, 1926, by E.P. Dutton & Co., Inc. Copyright renewed 1954 by A.A. Milne. Reprinted by permission of E.P. Dutton, McClelland and Stewart Limited, Toronto, and Curtis Brown Ltd., London. ● Poictesme © 1928 by Peacock Press/Argus Books. ● Hyborian Age copyright © 1950 by Gnome Press, Inc. Used by permission of David A. Kyle. ● Alimentary Canal © 1930 by George S. Chappell. ● Ernest H. Shepard's map of Toad Hall from *The Wind in the Willows* by Kenneth Grahame is reproduced by permission of Charles Scribner's Sons. Copyright 1933, 1953 Charles Scribner's Sons. ● Map of Middle-earth drawn and embellished by Pauline Baynes. Based on the cartography of J.R.R. and C.J.R. Tolkien. Copyright © 1970 by George Allen & Unwin Ltd. ● Middle-earth, Gondor and Mordor, and The Shire from *The Lord of the Rings* by J.R.R. Tolkien. Copyright © 1965 by J.R.R. Tolkien. Reprinted by permission of Houghton Mifflin Company. ● Thror's Map and Wilderland from *The Hobbit* by J.R.R. Tolkien. Copyright © 1966 by J.R.R. Tolkien. Reprinted by permission of Houghton Mifflin Company. ● Beleriand from *The Silmarillion* by J.R.R. Tolkien. Copyright © 1977 by George Allen & Unwin (Publishers) Ltd. Reprinted by permission of Houghton Mifflin Company. ● Ouroboros County from *The Worm Ouroboros* by E.R. Eddison, new introduction by Orville Prescott. Copyright, 1926; 1952 by E.P. Dutton & Co., Inc. Renewal, 1953 by Winifred Grace Eddison and Jean Gudrun Rucker. Reprinted by permission of E.P. Dutton. ● The Three Kingdoms from *Mistress of Mistresses* by E. R. Eddison. Copyright 1953 by E.P. Dutton & Co., Inc. Reprinted by permission of E.P. Dutton. ● Swallows and Amazons from the book *Swallows and Amazons*. Copyright 1931 by J.B. Lippincott Company. Copyright © renewed 1958 by Arthur Ransome. Reproduced by permission of J.B. Lippincott Company. ● Islandia from *The Islar* by Mark Saxton. Copyright © 1969 by Mark Saxton. Reprinted by permission of Houghton Mifflin Company. ● Raintree County and Waycross maps from *Raintree County* by Ross Lockridge. Copyright 1947 by Ross Lockridge, renewed © 1975 by Vernice Lockridge Noyes. Reprinted by permission of Houghton Mifflin Company. ● J.J. Boies' map of Narnia reproduced courtesy of J.J. Boies. ● C.S. Lewis' map of Narnia © n.d. by Trustees of the Estate of C.S. Lewis. ● Chronicles of Narnia map by Pauline Baynes. Copyright © 1972 by Penguin Books Ltd. Reprinted by permission of Penguin Books Ltd. ● Dalarna from *The Well of the Unicorn* by George U. Fletcher. Copyright © 1948 by William Sloane Associates. Copyright renewed 1976 by John Clark. Reproduced by permission of Curtis Brown Ltd. ● Map of Commonwealth from *Silverlock* by John Myers Myers. Copyright © 1949 by John Myers Myers. ● Neptune, Pluto, and Saturn © 1940 by Better Publications. ● Mars, Mercury, and Uranus © 1941 by Better Publications. ● Eros, Moon of Mars, Pirates' Planet, and Other Side of the Moon © 1942 by Better Publications. ● Aar and Twin Planets © 1943 by Better Publications. ● Futuria © 1944 by Better Publications. ● Mars from *The Best of Leigh Brackett*. Copyright © 1977 by Leigh Brackett. ● Land Between the Mountains map illustration by Erik Blegvad from *The Gammage Cup* © 1959 by Carol Kendall. Reproduced by permission of Harcourt Brace Jovanovich, Inc. ● Lower Slobbovia © 1948 by United Features Syndicate, Inc. ● Hyperborea © 1971 by Lin Carter. Reproduced by permission of Arkham House Publishers, Inc. Sauk City, Wisconsin 53583. ● Zothique used with permission of Mrs. L. Sprague de Camp. ● Quivera from *The City of Frozen Fire* by Vaughan Wilkins reprinted with permission of Macmillan Publishing Co., Inc. Copyright © 1951 by Vaughan Wilkins. ● Jefferson, Yoknapatawpha County, Mississippi from *Absalom! Absalom!*, by William Faulkner. Copyright 1936 and renewed 1964 by Estelle Faulkner and Jill Faulkner Summers. Reprinted with permission of Random House, Inc. ● Witch World map from *Witch World* by André Norton. Copyright © 1963 by Ace Books, Inc. Reprinted with permission of Grosset & Dunlap, Inc. ● Hi-lay Islands from *The Snouters* by Gerolf Steiner. Copyright © 1967 by Gustav Fisher Verlag. Reprinted by permission of Gustav Fisher Verlag. ● Earthsea from *A Wizard of Earthsea* by Ursula K. Le Guin. Copyright © 1968 by Ursula Le Guin. Reprinted by permission of Victor Gollancz Ltd. ● Lands Beyond from *The Phantom Tollbooth* by Norton Juster, illustrated by Jules Feiffer. Copyright © 1961 by Norton Juster and Jules Feiffer. Reprinted with permission of Random House, Inc., and William Collins Sons & Co., London. ● Og from *The Secret World of Og* by Pierre Berton. Copyright © 1962 by Pierre Berton. Reprinted by permission of Curtis Brown Ltd. ● Dilfar from *Warlocks and Warriors* by Roger Zelazny. Copyright © 1970 by L. Sprague de Camp. Reprinted by permission of Mrs. L. Sprague de Camp. ● The Young Kingdoms from *The Bane of the Black Sword*, *The Weird of the White Wolf*, *The Vanishing Tower*, and *Stormbringer* by Michael Moorcock. Copyright © 1963, 1965, 1967, 1977 by Michael Moorcock. Reprinted by permission of DAW Books, Inc. ● Grand Motholam from *The Dying Earth* by Jack Vance. Copyright © 1976 by George Barr and Tim Underwood. Used with the permission of Tim Underwood. ● Lankhmar by Tim Kirk, after Fritz Leiber. Copyright © 1963. Used with the permission of Tim Kirk. ● Prydain maps from *The Book of Three*, *The High King*, and *The Black Cauldron* by Lloyd Alexander, maps by Evaline Ness. Copyright © 1964, 1965, 1968 by Lloyd Alexander. Reproduced by permission of Holt, Rinehart & Winston, Inc. ● Lemuria maps reproduced by permission of Lin Carter. ● Dune map copyright © 1965 by Frank Herbert. Used with permission. ● The Severn Valley at Brichester from *The Inhabitant of the Lake* by J. Ramsey Campbell. Copyright © 1964 by J. Ramsey Campbell. Reprinted by permission of Arkham House Publishers, Inc. ● Mongo © 1974 by King Features Syndicate, Inc. ● Atlantis and Tyros from *Fantastic Swordsmen* by L. Sprague de Camp. Copyright © 1967 by L. Sprague de Camp. Reprinted by permission of Mrs. L. Sprague de Camp. ● Kanthos, Sulmannon, and Anzor from *Bane of Kanthos* by Alex Dain. Copyright © 1969 by Alex Dain. Reprinted by permission of Ace Books, Inc. ● Deryni from *Deryni Rising* by Katherine Kurtz. Copyright © 1970 by Katherine Kurtz. ● Pern from *The White Dragon* by Anne McCaffrey. Copyright © 1978 by Anne McCaffrey. ● Duchy of Strackenz from *Royal Flash*, by George MacDonald Fraser. Copyright © 1970 by George MacDonald Fraser. Reprinted by permission of Alfred A. Knopf, Inc. ● Dreamland from *Fantastic Swordsmen* by L. Sprague de Camp. Copyright © 1967 by L. Sprague de Camp. Reproduced courtesy of Mrs. L. Sprague de Camp. ● Arkham from *The Arkham Collector*, Summer 1970. Copyright © 1970 by August Derlath. Reprinted by permission of Arkham House Publishers, Inc. ● Mafrica © n.d. Jack Scruby. ● The Beklan Empire from *Shardik* by Richard Adams. Copyright © 1974 by Richard Adams. Reprinted by permission of Simon & Schuster, a Division of Gulf & Western Corporation. ● Florin and Guilder from *The Princess Bride* by William Goldman. Copyright © 1973 by William Goldman. ● Skaith maps from *The Ginger Star*, *The Hounds of Skaith*, and *The Reavers of Skaith* by Leigh Brackett. Copyright © 1974, 1976 by Leigh Brackett Hamilton. ● The Four Lands from *The Sword of Shannara* by Terry Brooks. Copyright © 1977 by Terry Brooks. Illustrations copyright © 1977 by Random House, Inc. ● The Land from *Lord Foul's Bane*, *The Illearth War*, and *The Power That Preserves* by Stephen R. Donaldson. Copyright © 1977 by Stephen R. Donaldson. Map copyright © 1977 by Lynn K. Plagge.

Introduction

A GUIDE TO WONDER

Lester del Rey

To the inner eye, all maps are filled with roads that lead to wonder and the dreams of fantasy. There is magic in the very names of places: Samarkand and Far Cathay, Hyderabad and Mandalay, Phundahl, Poictesme, Aquilonia, and South Ithilien. Only those hopelessly lost to romance can fail to be stirred.

Some places are real and some are imaginary. Those from the maps of our present world fade before the cold touch of reality; but those from the lands of fantasy remain ever new and fresh, untarnished by time or the uncertain promise of progress.

It may seem strange, at first thought, that there should be maps for lands that are only imaginary. But the author who seeks to travel through his world of fantasy is as much in need of a guide as is the one who charts a story of any other exploration. Without a map, his sense of time and distance soon becomes confused. Hence, many of the classic fantasies have been written by men who first drew up a reasonably detailed map of the realms about which they later created their fiction.

Certainly the reader of such tales is also in need of a map to help him follow the author through the course of the story. A good map brings the territory into sharp focus, giving it a sense of reality otherwise lacking. Without such a guide, the reader is often forced to attempt his own mental cartography, or to remain hopelessly vague about much of the development of the story.

For some unknown reason, many of the published classics of fantasy never included maps, even when the author had drawn them. Edgar Rice Burroughs sketched the details of his Mars and the strange lands that Tarzan traveled, but few of his books use them. Some more recent novels, such as the works of J. R. R. Tolkien, have excellent maps. But few readers of the Prydain novels of Lloyd Alexander know that a map is available. Austin Tappan Wright's *Islandia* included a map—but one that was almost illegible; yet a clear and detailed one was available elsewhere.

There was a need for such cartographic information, but for most people there was no ready source. Hard-pressed librarians were usually unable to help. Few libraries had the facilities to store and catalog such maps; and in many cases, no widely reproduced copies were available.

To answer this need, J. B. Post began compiling *An Atlas of Fantasy.* It was first published in 1973 and instantly became a classic work of reference. Five or more years later, it still remains unique as a reference book and a source of pleasure to all who love works of high imagination.

J. B. Post was perhaps the only person who could have undertaken and completed the enormous task of compiling this work. As the map librarian for the Free Library of Philadelphia, he had the training and the facilities to locate and obtain the necessary rare maps and scarce reproductions. And as a long-time reader of fantasy and science fiction, he had the understanding and love needed for the task. In the diverse fields of bibliography, maps, and the branches of fantasy, he is a recognized authority.

The result was an outstanding work—a true classic, as I have said. Yet there were limits to what could be done at the time. Some maps were available only in reproductions that made clear copying difficult. Others were simply not available. And, of course, during the last few years the sudden resurgence of interest in fantasy has produced many new maps that should be included.

Now, fortunately, there is a new edition in new format, and made more available at a lower price. There has been time and opportunity to work on the *Atlas* again.

I am delighted and happy to have this chance to introduce the new edition to the larger audience it can serve so well. My original, hardcover edition—which I bought when I first saw it—has begun to show wear from repeated usage. And while I have much of the new material available, I shall now be able to find it readily in a single source, rather than hunting desperately.

As a reference work, I consider this to be one of the most valuable—if, indeed, not *the* most valuable—books on fantasy ever published.

But that's only a small part of my reason for wanting a copy of this new edition for itself. When it appears, I shall sit quietly leafing through it, reading the notes and staring at those marvelous maps of the lands I have visited in my mind. And once again I shall be lost among names and places of wonder.

A map, as the semanticists tell us, is not the territory, as a symbol is not the entity. But magic has never accepted this; in the worlds of magic, the symbol controls and dominates. And a map of one of those worlds can open the territory beyond the power of words to describe.

Minas Tirith, Zodanga, and the Valley of Jad-Ben-Otho; Storisende and Koshtra Pivrarcha; Cimmeria, Dalarna, and the Kargad Lands! Here, with small apologies to Keats, are indeed magic casements, opening on the foam of sorcerous seas, in fairy lands reborn.

Preface to the Ballantine Edition

Having a book published is much like having an argument; for several nights one stares at the ceiling and mutters "I should have said . . ." If life gives us few chances to replay an argument, it is on some occasions more generous with books. But even when one has a chance for a new edition with additions, deletions, and corrections, one still stares at the ceiling wishing one had done things differently.

This time around for *An Atlas of Fantasy* some of the less inspired maps and most of the poor quality ones have been dropped. Others have been rephotographed. While some of those added were available when the first edition was compiled, many represent new maps drawn since 1972. Some maps continue to elude us for the same reasons as before: money, permissions, and availability. Well, we can always hope for *Another Atlas of Fantasy;* the maps are there, we just need the interest.

While most of the philosophical matters pertaining to fantasy maps are discussed in the following essay, "On Charting Unreal Realms," which first appeared in the Mirage edition, there is one point I feel needs some elaboration: the "one-to-one" map. Just as we do not include cartograms because they attempt to show a statistical "reality" rather than a spatial one, I feel that a map such

as one showing Thomas Hardy's imaginary countryside, "Wessex," is also inappropriate to a fantasy atlas, though not to a literary one. Hardy took the south of England and merely renamed it. On the maps I have seen, it is not merely that a real place inspired a Wessex locale, it *is* that locale. When only the names have been changed, that is not sufficient. If the geography of the "real" world is used but a parallel world's political structure is imposed on it, that map is a candidate because there is some fantasy element about it (the world of H. Beam Piper's *Lord Kalvan of Otherwhen* is a prime example, but I have yet to find a map for it).

The thanks extended in the Mirage edition of course hold for this edition as well. Two additional special mentions must be made, however: the management of the Philadelphia branch of B. Dalton was kind enough not to throw me out when I spent entire days reading novels in their bookstore; and Lynne Williams Bair and Carolyn Hart, my editors at Ballantine, are the persons primarily responsible for the actual existence of this new edition.

Again, in this edition, the emphasis is on what one traditionally classes as science fiction and fantasy. My mystery and detective story reading friends have given me enough suggestions to put together *The Detectives' Handy Pocket Atlas,* but they'll have to wait for that, I fear. The ever growing interest in fantasy has inspired most publishers to want maps in their major books if for no other reason than maps are now becoming fashionable, and because "Tolkien has them." While one may disparage shallow imitation, it has led to more maps appearing in books, surely a worthy result.

Just as there is no end to mapping the real world, there is no end to mapping worlds of imagination. Citations (or, better yet, copies) of any maps I seem to have missed, or which will be published in the future, will always be welcome, as will any suggestions for improvement. And now while you, I hope, enjoy the following pages, I shall go off in the corner and mutter "I should have done it this way . . ."

J. B. Post
Philadelphia, Pa.
May 18, 1978

On Charting Unreal Realms

Maps of imaginary lands have been with us a long time. Essentially they are of two kinds: geographical speculation and literary fabrication. While the maps which most concern us in this book spring from literary fabrication, no category really holds up eternally. As Post's Postulate states, "pigeon holes are only good for pigeons." We will find that rigid definitions break down all too soon and we must be flexible in what we mean by "map" and "imaginary." Still, this book is not meant to be a look at the entire universe of cartographic fantasy. Cartographic fantasy can be defined as those maps which are nonrepresentational of the "real" world in approved ways. Many maps are not meant to be geographically representative and often confuse some viewers; as an example, maps showing the relation between the population of the various states of the Union by size of the state on the map are still tied to objective statistics. Aside from maps of imaginary lands, cartographic fantasy includes maps from the lore of various cults which have distinct geographical beliefs, maps from the world of advertising (remember "the Atlantic River" map for TWA?), disproportionate maps, the "might have been" maps showing the war aims of the losing side, and the completely decorative map. A sample of such maps may be seen in the first number of *The Map Collectors' Circle* wherein R. V. Tooley shows us "Geographical Oddities." The common denominator of all of these maps is an ulterior motive—a motive other than geographical (in the broadest meaning of the term) representation of the "real" world. The definitive study of cartographic fantasy remains to be written—the title "Fantasia Cartographica" should be used when it is—but in the meantime we offer a brief survey of one portion of the field.

Even in the subfield of maps of imaginary lands derived from literary sources the choices are vast. Obviously this book is not intended to be exhaustive: our title, *An Atlas of Fantasy*, admits the possibility of another atlas of fantasy (and more than one more) being produced in the future if demand warrants it. At the outset let me admit that my sins of omission in this volume are infinite. Please don't ask "Why didn't you include . . . ?" Some of the obvious maps not included are a map of Moomin Valley, the map from Alan Garner's *The Weirdstone,* a map of Neverland, a map of Graustark, a map of Akenfield, a map of the Ponderosa Ranch, and a map of the Village from the television show "The Prisoner." The reasons for exclusion have been varied but generally have been too high a permission fee for reproduction rights, denial of permission, the poor quality of the original map, the inability to locate a copy of the map, the inability technically to reproduce the map and still keep the cost per volume within some kind of reason, the nonexistence of a map of certain imaginary lands, the general similarity between certain maps, or the fact that the story was set in a real place.

In any project of this sort many hands are involved, hands without whom I would not have been able to offer this selection to the world. First and foremost are the artists, living and dead, who drew the maps. Next, recognition must be rendered to the many publishers who permitted the maps to be reproduced. Thanks must go to that nameless and faceless horde of well wishers who kept asking "Do you know about . . . ?" even when I knew about the map they suggested; their interest and concern kept me going through some bad times. Special thanks must be offered to very special people: to Joyce just for being my wife but also for much leg work; to Richard Stephenson of the Library of Congress, my peer in the study of cartographic fantasy, for encouragement; to L. Sprague de Camp for unhesitating generosity; to Lin Carter for generosity and much good advice; to Hulbert Burroughs for the unpublished Edgar Rice Burroughs material; to Gary Labowitz for the loan of a real treasure; to Oswald Train for valuable suggestions and the generous loan of much material; to Lt. Col. George Scithers for permissions, material, and a loan; to Linda Fein for help with the children's books; and to Jack Chalker and Bill Osten for publishing our collective efforts.

Where not otherwise noted, the maps are from the Map Collection of the Free Library of Philadelphia.

The last "thank you" is to you, the reader; for, without readers, what use is a book?

J. B. Post
Philadelphia, Pa.
October 2, 1972

Contents

An Atlas
of Fantasy

EDEN

Theological and archaeological speculation combine in the
search for Eden and a description of its geography. This map was
made circa 776 by Spanish monks and illustrates the state of
geographical knowledge at that time. For those who read German,
Richard Hennig's *Wo Lag das Paradies* (Berlin: Verlag des
Druckhaus Tempelhof, 1950) from which this map was taken, is an
interesting study in the search for Paradise.

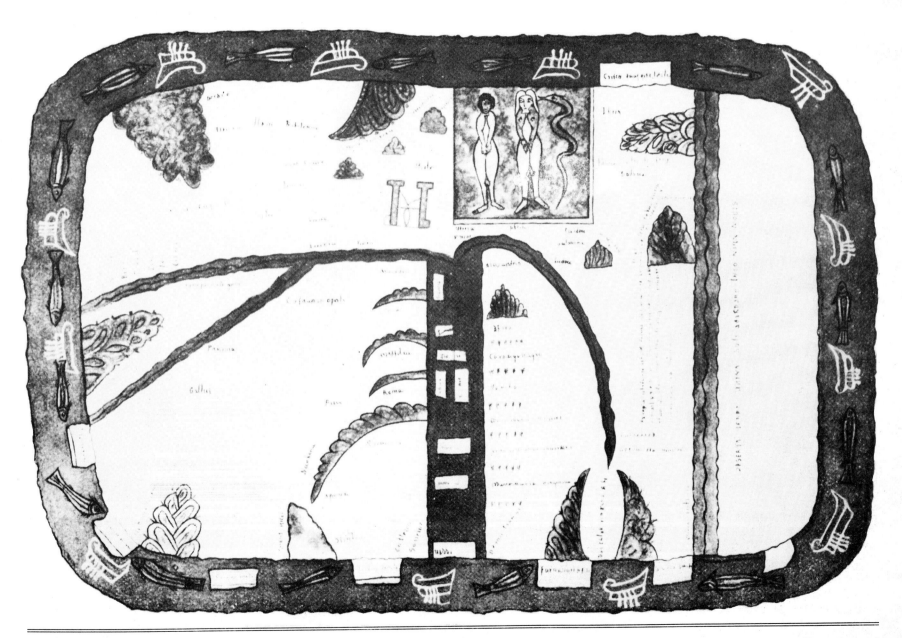

ATLANTIC OCEAN AND THE AZORES

As European geographical knowledge increased maps became fairly accurate for known lands, but for areas not yet fully explored information was incomplete or contradictory. Mapmakers did the best they could, but hearsay, compounded in part by outright fraud, honest error in sighting, and garbled reporting, soon populated the Atlantic Ocean with innumerable islands, most of them ghosts. Strictly speaking these maps fall under the general heading of geographical speculation, but one or two samples should at least be included. The maps here are actually modern redrawings—the originals being difficult to reproduce—taken from Samuel Eliot Morison's *The European Discovery of America* (New York: Oxford University Press, 1971).

For a more detailed study of this whole matter, see William H. Babcock's *Legendary Islands of the Atlantic: A Study in Medieval Geography* (New York: American Geographical Society, 1922), Samuel Eliot Morison's "Flyaway Islands and False Voyages 1100–1492" in his *The European Discovery of America: The Northern Voyages A.D. 500–1600* (New York: Oxford University Press, 1971), and Raymond Ramsay's *No Longer on the Map* (New York: Viking Press, 1972).

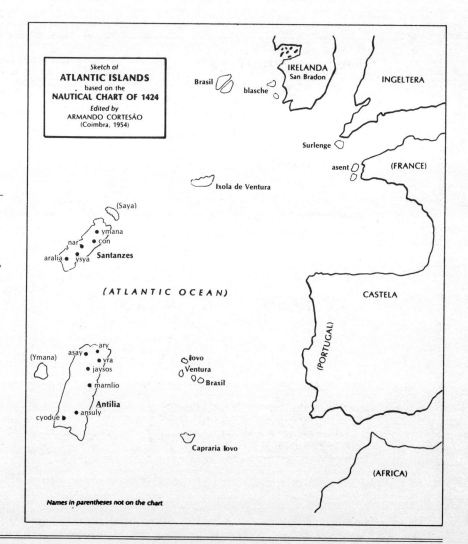

Sketch of
ATLANTIC ISLANDS
based on the
NAUTICAL CHART OF 1424
Edited by
ARMANDO CORTESÃO
(Coimbra, 1954)

Names in parentheses not on the chart

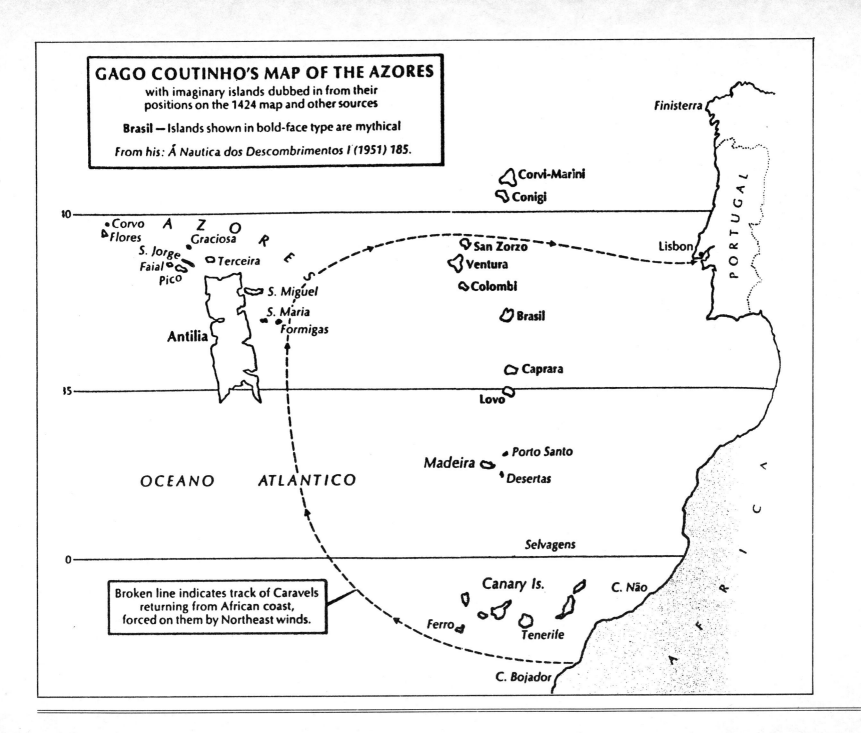

GAGO COUTINHO'S MAP OF THE AZORES

with imaginary islands dubbed in from their
positions on the 1424 map and other sources

Brasil — Islands shown in bold-face type are mythical

From his: *Á Nautica dos Descombrimentos I (1951) 185.*

Finisterra

Corvi-Marini

Conigi

40

Corvo A Z O R E S

Flores Graciosa

San Zorzo

Lisbon

S. Jorge

Faial Terceira

Ventura

Pico

PORTUGAL

S. Miguel

Colombi

S. Maria

Brasil

Antilia

Formigas

Caprara

35

Lovo

Madeira Porto Santo

OCEANO ATLANTICO

Desertas

Selvagens

0

Canary Is. C. Não

Broken line indicates track of Caravels
returning from African coast,
forced on them by Northeast winds.

Ferro Tenerife

A F R I C A

C. Bojador

UTOPIA

Thomas More's *Utopia* gave a new word to the language and reintroduced a concept to European thought. The faraway (in time or space, or both) place where things were more perfect than the-here-and-now had been used by the Greeks. Christianity transformed the perfection of utopia into the wonders of the afterlife. Thomas More reintroduced the more perfect worldly locale in 1516, and we have had its like ever since. The mirror–image concept, the "dystopia," depicts places less perfect than the world we know. While each can be entertaining in its own right, the general purpose of each is to preach about the evils and ills of the here-and-now either by holding up the model of utopia to show current deficiencies, or by depicting a dystopia and direly predicting it as our fate "if this goes on."

The city of Amaurotum, based largely on More's descriptions. The drawings show (A) the site plan, (B) the possible elevation, and (C) the situation of the city in relation to the drainage system. Market areas are shaded.

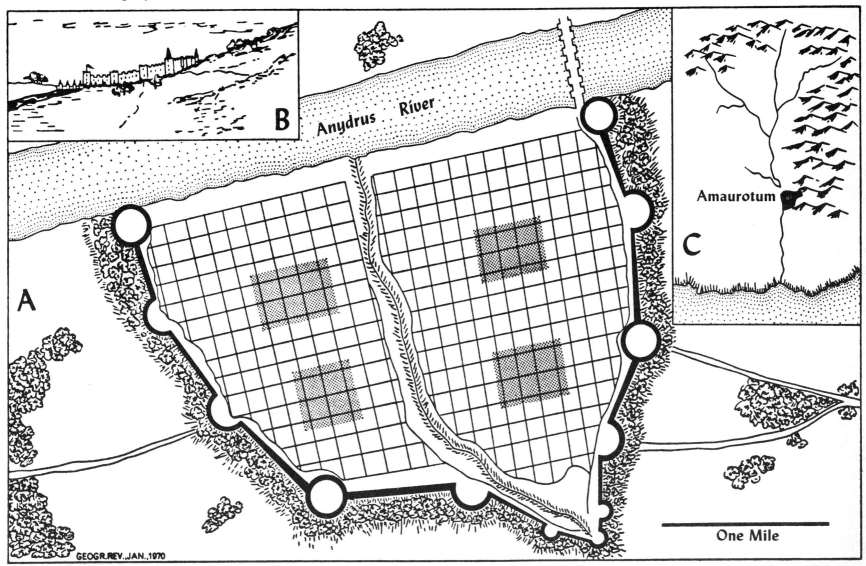

B

Anydrus River

Amaurotum

C

A

GEOGR.REV.,JAN.,1970

One Mile

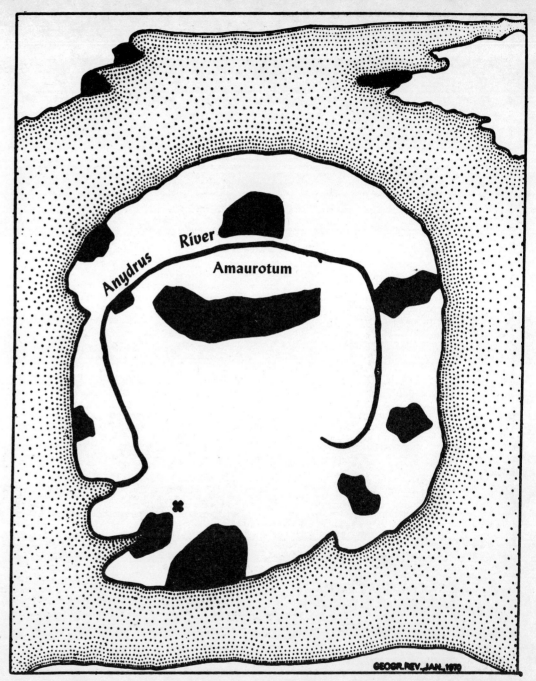

Map of Utopia based on the woodcut of 1518,
a foreshortened pictogram with urban elevations.
Here the urban areas are represented by shading.

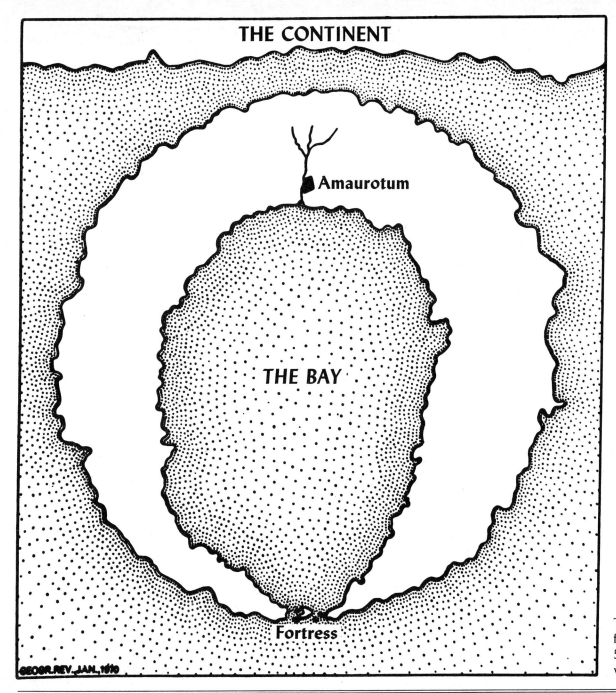

THE CONTINENT

Amaurotum

THE BAY

Fortress

GEOGR. REV. JAN. 1910

This outline represents one possible form for Utopia. Here the circumference of 500 miles is preserved and the broadest width, 200 miles, is lost.

SCHLARAFFENLANDE

Schlaraffenlande was a famous utopia in German literature.
Related to the Cocaigne of English and French literature,
Schlaraffenlande also had roasted pigs walking about the streets
with knives stuck into them so the lazy inhabitants of the land
merely had to eat at what walked past. All the necessities and
luxuries of life literally fell into one's lap. This map is reproduced
from a copy in the Library of Congress.

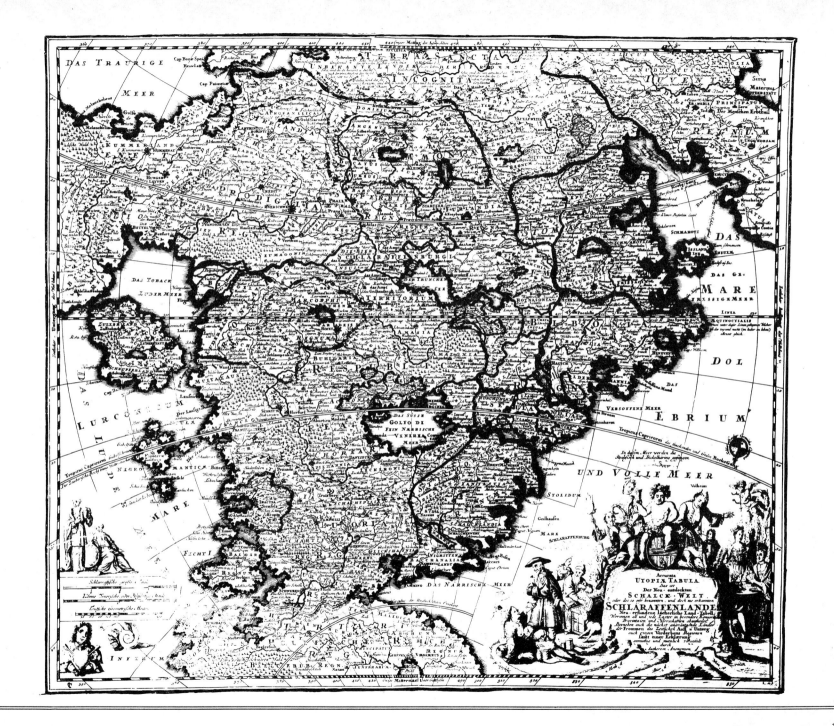

HELL

Students of literature will recall the excellent map—more precisely, diagram—of Hell accompanying the John Ciardi translation of Dante's *Inferno*. Instead of that familiar one, here is a far less known—but equally interesting—map of Hell drawn by Eugene Cox in 1928 depicting the Hell of John Milton.

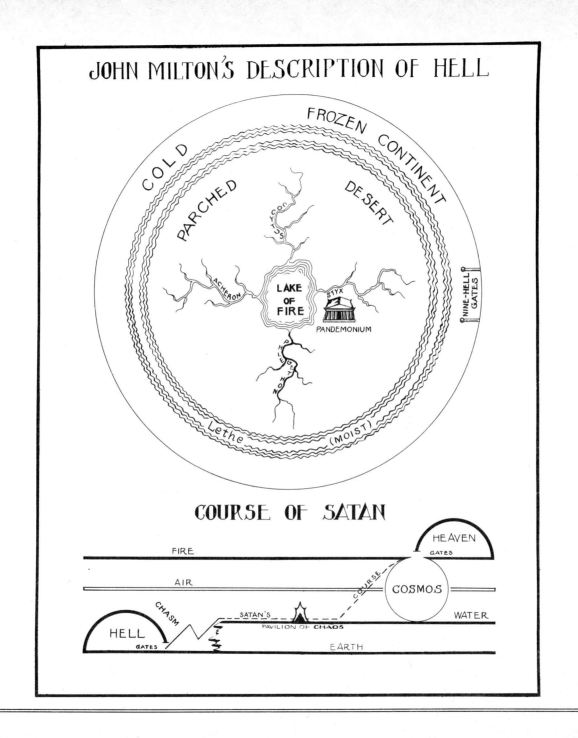

MAPPA GEOGRAPHIAE NATURALIS

The German *didaktische karte* (literally, "teaching map") has essentially two functions: to teach the new maker of maps the cartographic conventions and to teach the user of maps the same conventions. A map becomes a true representation of the Earth's surface rather than just a pretty collection of colors and symbols. This map was drawn about 1730 by Matthaus Seutter (1678—1757).

The reader of German, so my German-reading friends tell me, will be able to detect all sorts of puns on the map. The use of puns is quite common on this kind of map; in fact, there seem to be only three possible ways to label a map illustrating cartographic conventions: unimaginatively calling features by their generic name (city, town, river, peninsula, etc.); drawing from literature (Barchester, Graustark, etc.); or creating new names, usually a play on words (Rock Sound, Generation Gap, Cape Crusader, etc.). Recently Bradford Thomas of Kent State University's Department of Geography produced a "Map of Traphique Island" loaded with some of the worst puns I have ever seen.

ATTACK
OF LOVE

Also by Matthaus Seutter is this map showing the attack of love upon the heart. It is reproduced from a copy of the second volume of his *Atlas Novus*, circa 1745, owned by the Library of Congress. Unfortunately, this map is very difficult to reproduce, and much of the clarity is lost here. The text of the map is in both French and German and describes methods of defending the heart against attacks of love, as well as the attacking positions. I'll put my money on the offensive.

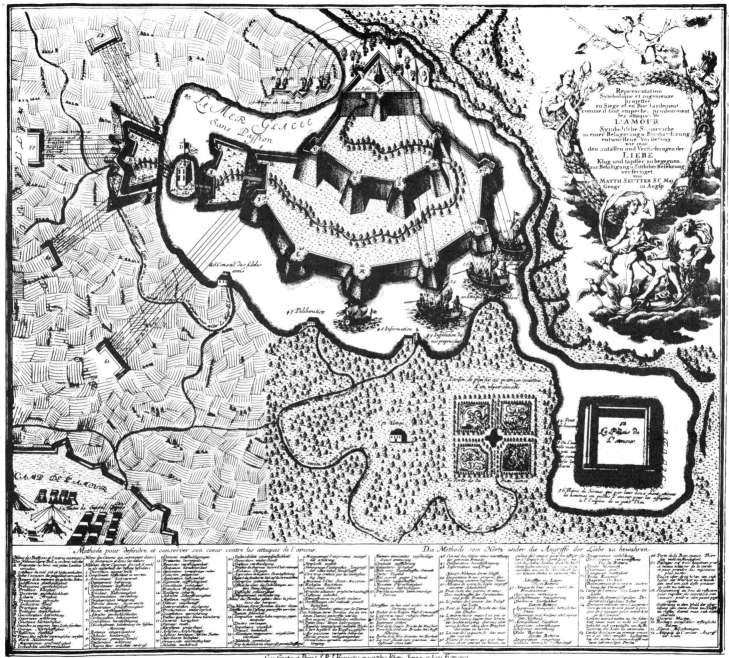

PILGRIM'S PROGRESS

John Bunyan's *Pilgrim's Progress* is an allegorical tale of the trials
and tribulations of a chap named Christian as he flees the wrath
of the Lord. He carries a load of sins on his back until he reaches
the Place of Deliverance. Each place and event is grossly symbolic
of Christian beliefs. Characters are named "Christian," "Evangalist,"
"Pliable," and so forth; places have such names as "Vanity Fair,"
"City of Destruction," "Doubting Castle," etc. *Pilgrim's Progress* is
the most famous allegorical journey, and this map by Robert
Lawson for the 1939 Lippincott reprinting of the Mary Godolphin
retelling (1884) can stand as representative of a whole class of
allegorical maps.

PILGRIM'S PROGRESS

ZION

HOUSE
BEAUTIFUL

DESTRUCTION

LAND OF BEULAH

DIFFICULTY

SPRING
OF LIFE

DANGER

WICKET GATE

INTERPRETER'S
HOUSE

VALE OF
HUMILIATION

MORALITY

FORT OF
BEELZEBUB

ENCHANTED
GROUND

VALLEY OF THE
THE SHADOW OF DEATH

VANITY FAIR

CONCEIT

SLOUGH OF
DESPOND

CLEAR

ERROR

BY PATH
MEADOW

THE CITY OF
DESTRUCTION

DELECTABLE
MOUNTAINS

DOUBTING
CASTLE

VOYAGES OF LEMUEL GULLIVER

Chronicled by Jonathan Swift (1665–1745), the travels of Lemuel
Gulliver into divers parts of the world exercise a fascination upon
readers young and old. At one level they are entertaining travel
stories of the tall tale variety; at another level they are political and
social allegories poking fun at the British government. The maps
mean more in the context of the story, but for map fanciers there
are some items of intrinsic interest. This is not the place for a
complete cartobibliography, but it is worth noting that there have
been numerous discrepancies. For instance, in these maps from a
1766 edition of the novel there is no mountain range between
Brobdingnag and North America, but a 1730 French edition shows
one. Anyone concerned with the supposed location of Lilliput et al.
can consult the map in *Gulliver's Travel Notes* (Lincoln, Nebr.:
Cliff's Notes, 1969) which places Houyhnhnms Lands south of
South Africa, Lilliput west of Australia, Brobdingnag attached to
Alaska, and Laputa near Japan.

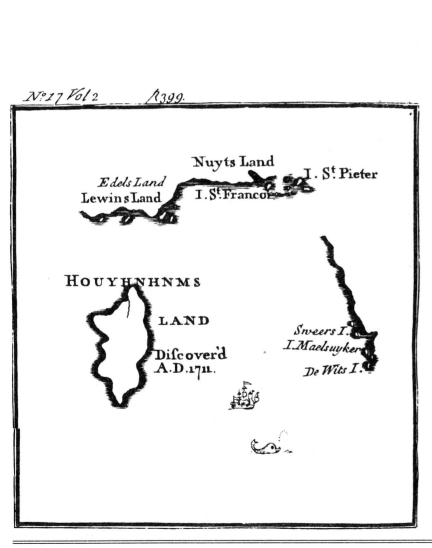

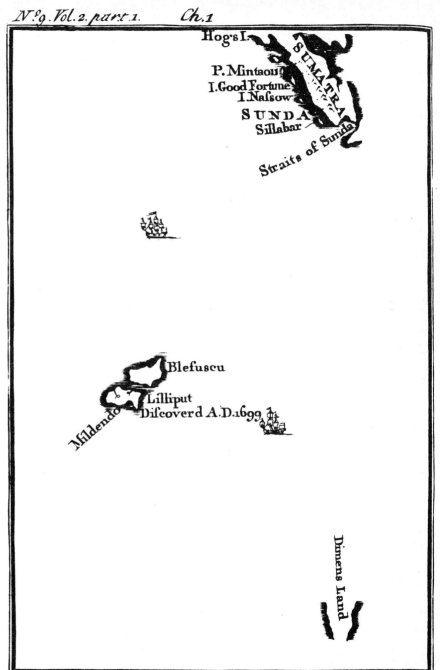

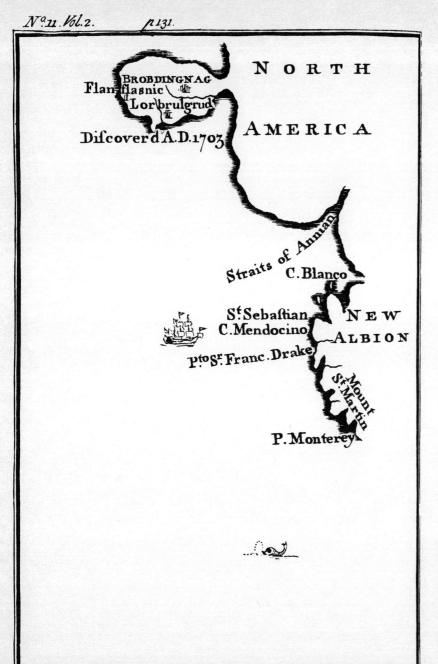

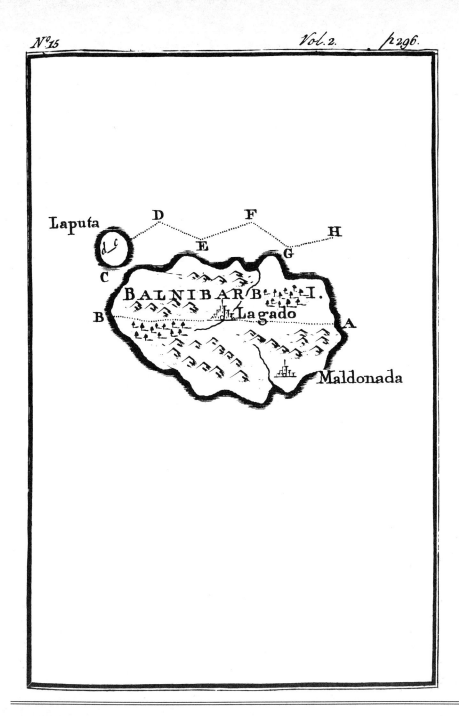

ALLESTONE

Allestone was the imaginary land created by Thomas Williams
Malkin (1795–1802). He was a precocious little boy who learned to
read and write early and who amused himself by writing stories.
After a painful illness he died, at the age of six. Intellectuals in those
days—even very young ones—were viewed with deep distrust.
Because people suspected the boy was physically damaged from
birth, his parents had an autopsy performed by a Dr. Lister, the
attending physician. The conclusion was death due to "inflamed
bowels," no congenital defect was found.

A calendar and dating system, a history and culture, and a
geography were created for Allestone. The stories may read a bit
crudely but consider that they were written by a six-year-old child.
One wonders what he might have done had he lived.

His father, Benjamin Heath Malkin, wrote *A Father's Memoirs
of His Child* (London: Longman, Hurst, Rees & Orme, 1806) which
tells of the brief life of Thomas Malkin. William Blake illustrated the
book. Appended to the biography is this map of Allestone and all
the Allestone stories.

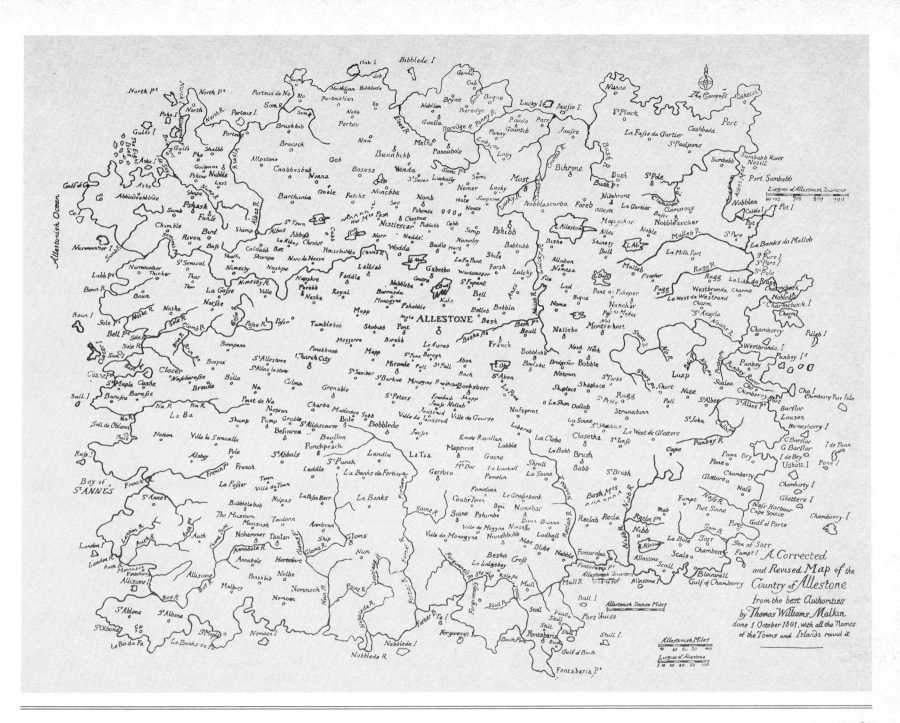

A Corrected and Revised Map of the Country of Allestone from the best Authorities by Thomas Williams Malkin done 1 October 1801 with all the Names of the Towns and Islands round it

ROAD
TO HELL

Returning to roads to Hell, we have a very interesting and rare, if almost unreadable, one. Drawn in 1858 by I. N. Barreton for Joseph Sightler, the original is in the Library of Congress. Note the major rivers: Gambling River, Drunkenness River, and Perdition River all have appropriate tributaries; Chess Creek, Backgammon Branch, Lottery Creek, Egg Nog Creek, Cider Branch, Lemonade Branch, Brandy Creek, Cheating Creek, Revenge Creek, Hatred Creek, etc. The quickest way to the Great Lake of Fire and Brimstone is by the Suicide Rail Road and the Duelist's Rail Road. One can meander along the road but shortcuts are provided for liars, drunkards, gamblers, and perjurors. All, however, finally go "blip" into the Great Lake. Not shown is the road to Heaven called "the Path of Ennui."

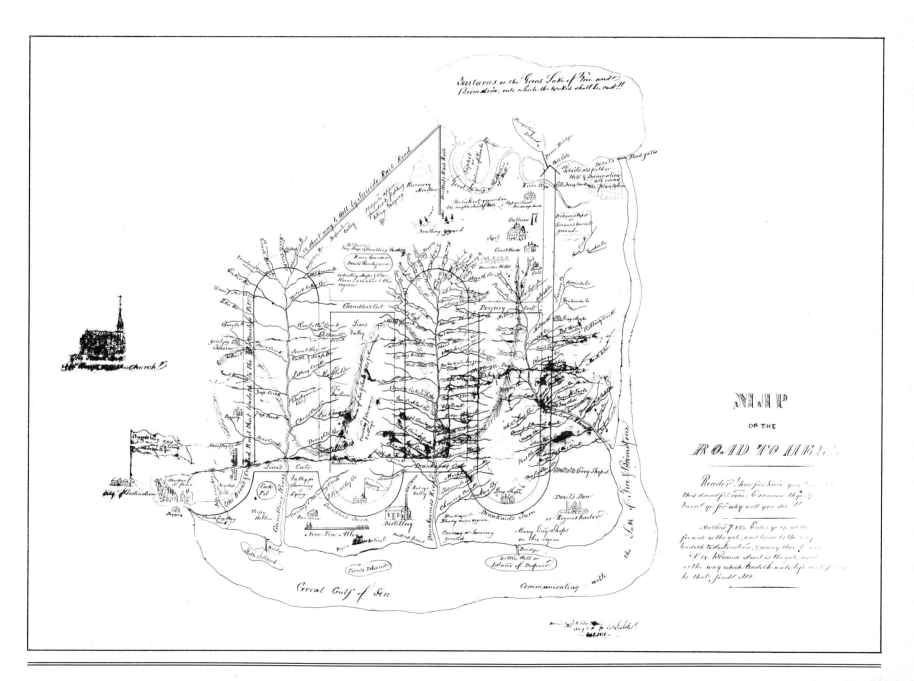

MAP

OF THE

ROAD TO HELL

BARSETSHIRE

One of the more famous imaginary lands is Barsetshire, England. Anthony Trollope (1815–1882) chronicled the doings of the good people around Barchester in his writings. The town itself was supposedly inspired by a trip to Salisbury—it has grown into a world of its own. In more recent times Angela Thirkell has continued the story of Barchester. The Maurice Weightman map appears as the endpaper decoration in Miss Thirkell's novel *Jutland Cottage* (New York: Alfred A. Knopf, 1953). The other maps are taken from *A Guide to Trollope* (Princeton: Princeton University Press, 1948) by Winifred and James Gerould, and were drawn by Florence W. Ewing. On the Weightman map note such places as Winter Overcotes and Winter Underclose.

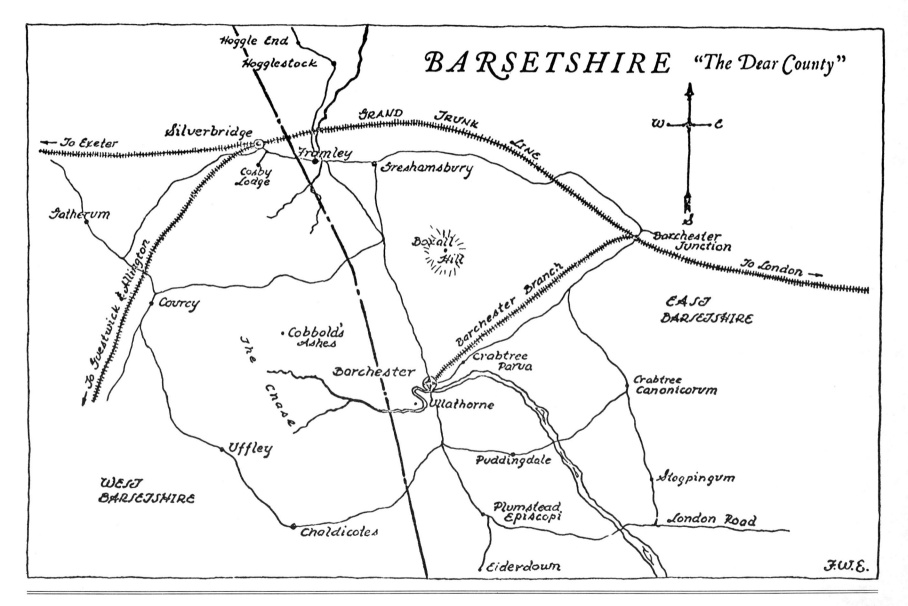

BARSETSHIRE "The Dear County"

Hoggle End
Hogglestock

GRAND TRUNK LINE

Silverbridge
To Exeter
Framley
Cosby Lodge
Greshamsbury
Gatherum
Boxall Hill
Darchester Junction
To London →

To Guestwick & Allington
Courcy
Barchester Branch
EAST BARSETSHIRE

The Chase
Cobbold's Ashes
Barchester
Crabtree Parva
Crabtree Canonicorum

Ullathorne
Uffley
Puddingdale
Stogpingum

WEST BARSETSHIRE
Plumstead Episcopi
London Road

Chaldicotes

Eiderdown

F.W.E.

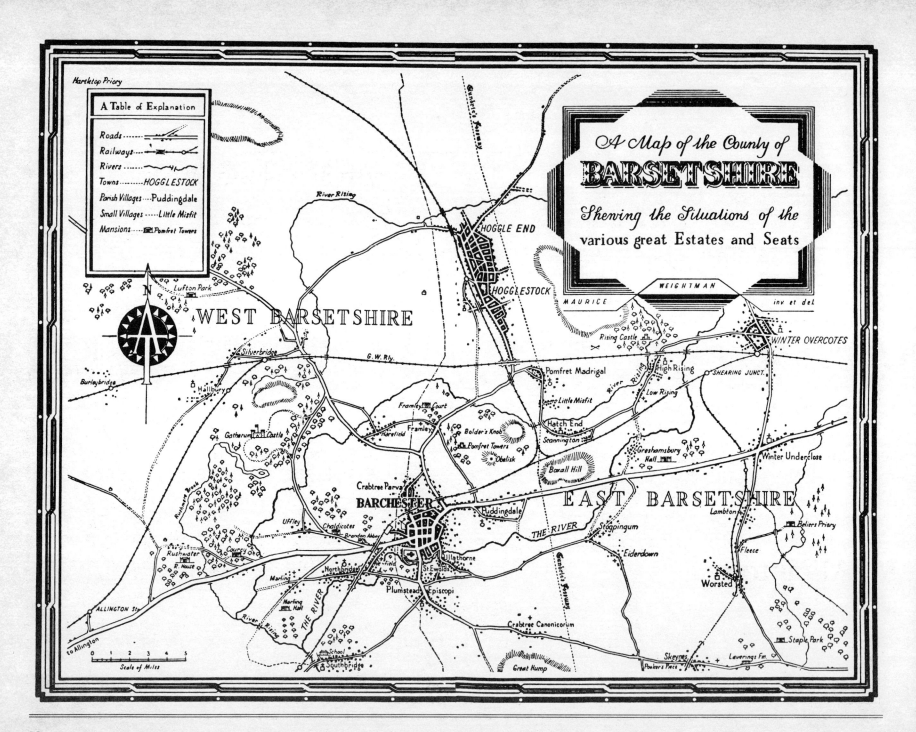

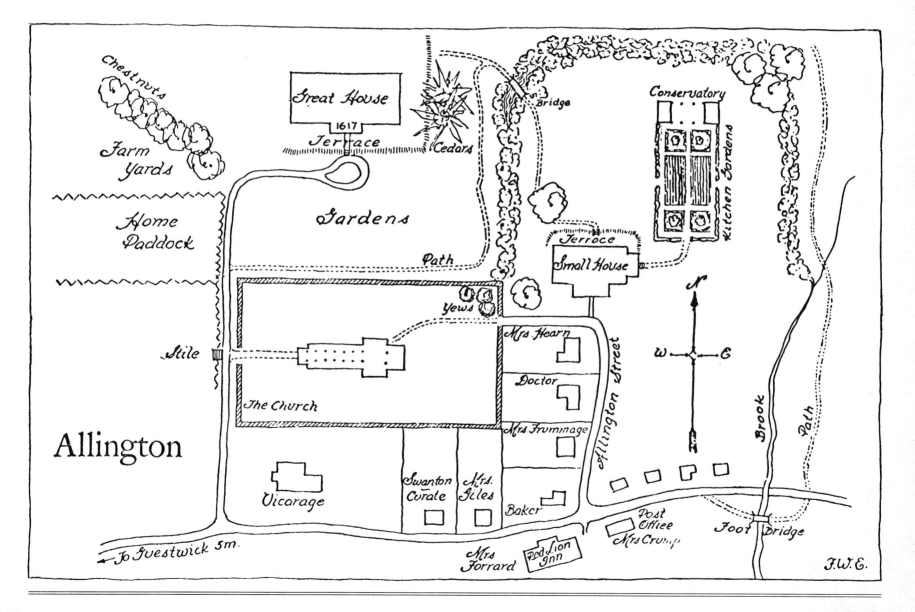

Chestnuts

Farm Yards

Home Paddock

Great House

1617

Terrace

Gardens

Cedars

Bridge

Path

Conservatory

Kitchen Gardens

Terrace

Small House

N

W E

Stile

Yews

Mrs. Hearn

Doctor

Mrs Frummage

Allington Street

The Church

Allington

Swanton Curate

Mrs. Giles

Baker

Brook

Path

Vicarage

Post Office

Mrs Crump

To Guestwick 5m.

Mrs Forrard

Red Lion Inn

Foot Bridge

F.W.E.

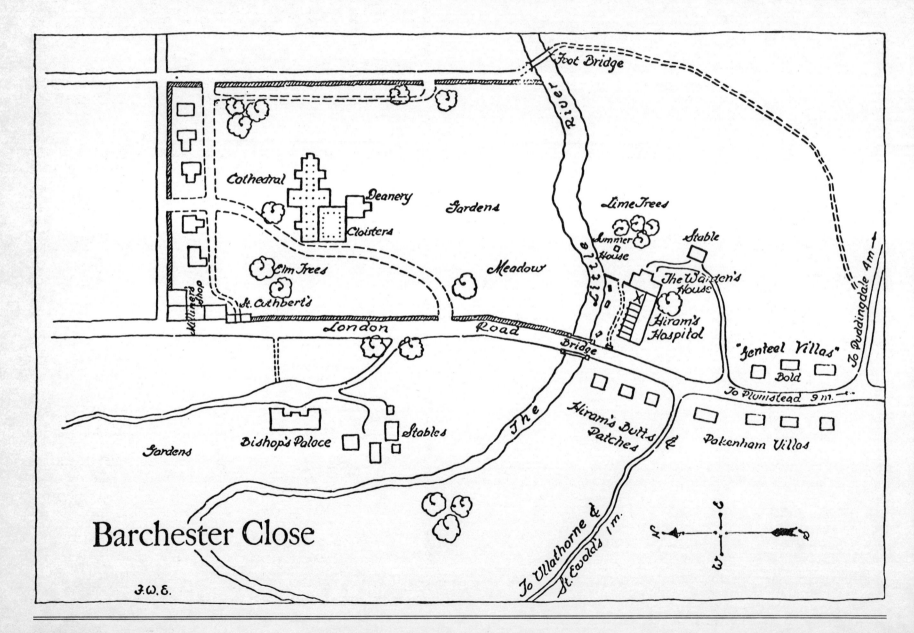

Barchester Close

Foot Bridge

Cathedral

Deanery

Cloisters

Gardens

Lime Trees

Summer House

Stable

Elm Trees

Meadow

The Warden's House

St. Cuthbert's

Hiram's Hospital

Milliner's Shop

London   Road

Bridge

"Genteel Villas"

Bold

To Puddingdale 4 m.

To Plumstead 9 m.

Gardens

Bishop's Palace

Stables

Hiram's Butts & Patches

Pakenham Villas

River Little

To Ullathorne & St. Ewold's 1 m.

The

F. W. E.

WORLD OF SHERLOCK HOLMES

Strictly speaking the imaginary journeyings of fictional characters in real places is not the proper subject matter for an atlas of fantasy. Once again, however, I am letting personal inclination override philosophical principles. Dartmoor is, of course, a real place in England. This map of the area around Baskerville Hall, scene of the exploits of Mr. Sherlock Holmes in the matter of *The Hound of the Baskervilles*, is from Julian Wolff's *The Sherlockian Atlas* (New York: privately printed, 1952), a fascinating little volume of thirteen plates charting the adventures of the Master. It is reproduced with the gracious permission of Dr. Wolff, as is the map of the trip to Reichenbach Falls.

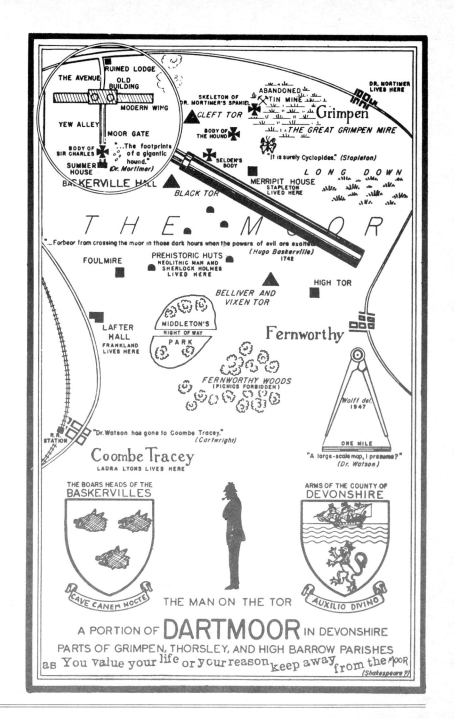

MAP OF MATRIMONY

Designed for "timid lovers," this map pretty well speaks for itself. One must avoid River Drain Purse, and Paymoney Point is shown beyond the Land of Lawyers. After all the dangers one finds Cape Delight and other such places. The map is reproduced from a copy in the Library of Congress.

MAP OF A GREAT COUNTRY

In an entirely different vein we have maps that attempt to show the way to better living. Since the road to salvation or perdition differs with each religion and sect, the possibilities for maps like this are almost endless. One must assume that "Great Country" lies south of the Demarcation Mountains, though many of my friends would consider such places as Whiskey Lake, Brothelburgh, and Drunken Hollow to be in a great country. Note that there are ways through the Demarcation Mountains. Two lines of the Temperance Rail Road run from the Territory of Indulgence and terminate in Friendly City and Charity. One can pass through the Straits of Total Abstinence from the Sea of Anguish into the Sea of Temperance, but can very easily be sucked through Temptation Straits through the Gulf of Broken Pledges past Despair and into the Gulf of Perdition.

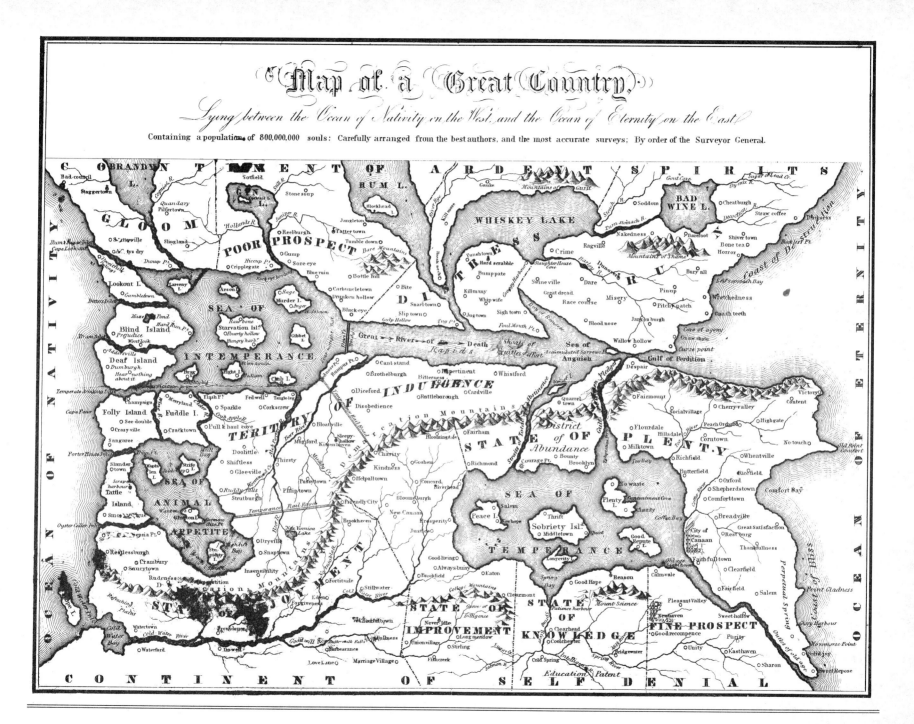

Map of a Great Country,

Lying between the Ocean of Nativity on the West, and the Ocean of Eternity on the East.

Containing a population of 800,000,000 souls: Carefully arranged from the best authors, and the most accurate surveys; By order of the Surveyor General.

TREASURE ISLAND

Ah! what boy has not thrilled to the adventures of Jim Hawkins seeking pirate treasure? Treasure Island was actually charted and laid out, and the map drawn, before the story was written. This is quite a common procedure with writers—it is somewhat embarrassing to go North to a city which was described as South in the first chapter—to help them remember the settings for their stories. In the case of *Treasure Island* the geography of the island influenced much of the action. Robert Louis Stevenson admitted that the reason the "Hispaniola" went wandering was because the island had two harbors.

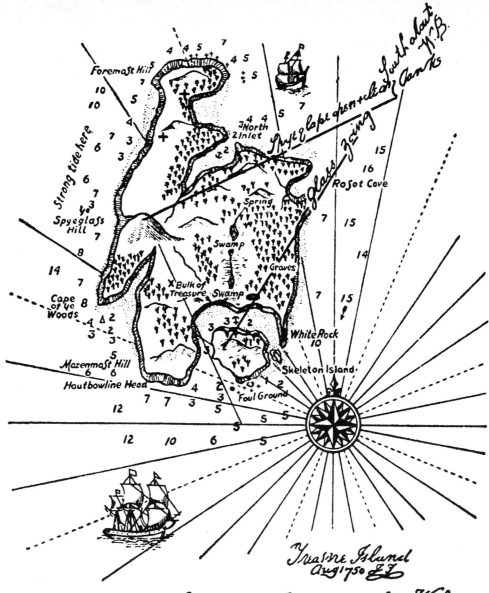

Foremast Hill

Strong tide here

Spyeglass Hill

Cape of ye Woods

Mazenmast Hill

Houtbowline Head

North Inlet

Spring

Swamp

Graves

X Bulk of Treasure

Swamp

Rofot Cove

White Rock

Skeleton Island

Foul Ground

Treasure Island
Aug 1750 J F

Given by above J. F. & Mr. W. Bones Maste of ye Walrus
Savannah this twenty July 1754 W. B.

Facsimile of Chart, latitude and
longitude struck out by J Hawkins

MYSTERIOUS ISLAND

Lincoln Island, in Jules Verne's novel *Mysterious Island,* is the stage for the adventures of Cyrus Harding, Gideon Spilett, Herbert Pencroft, and Neb, who arrive on March 25, 1865. With indomitable Yankee drive and skill, they transform the wilderness isle into a pleasant place to live. Luck, in the form of debris which they can salvage, seems to be on their side. At the end they discover they have been helped by Captain Nemo, whose submarine is trapped in an underground grotto.

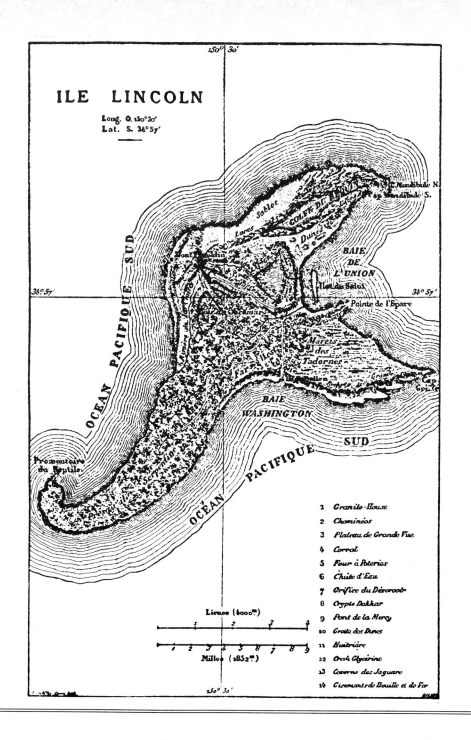

ILE LINCOLN

Long. O. 150°30'
Lat. S. 38°57'

OCÉAN PACIFIQUE SUD

GOLFE DU REQUIN

BAIE
DE
L'UNION

Sables
Laves
Dunes

Mont Franklin

Pointe de l'Épave

Marais
des
Tadornes

BAIE
WASHINGTON

OCÉAN PACIFIQUE SUD

Promontoire
du Reptile

1   Granite-House
2   Cheminées
3   Plateau de Grande Vue
4   Corral
5   Four à Poteries
6   Chute d'Eau
7   Orifice du Déversoir
8   Crypte Dakkar
9   Pont de la Mercy
10 Grotte des Dunes
11 Huitrière
12 Creek Glycérine
13 Caverne des Jaguars
14 Gisements de Houille et de Fer

Lieues (4000ᵐ)
1   2   3

Milles (1852ᵐ)

38°57'

150° 30'

CHAIRMAN ISLAND

Seventeen boys and a few adults are shipwrecked when the steamer "Severn" goes down in midocean. The boys were on a vacation from the Chairman School in Aukland. Naming the island after their school, they settle down to survival. The veneer of civilization begins to crack down and one has a vague prefiguring of Golding's *Lord of the Flies,* but adults finally arrive on the scene to unite the factions. Jules Verne's *A Long Vacation* (New York: Holt, Rinehart & Winston, 1967), from which this map is taken, is the usual Verne adventure tale: implausible but nicely tied up at the end and most enjoyable to read.

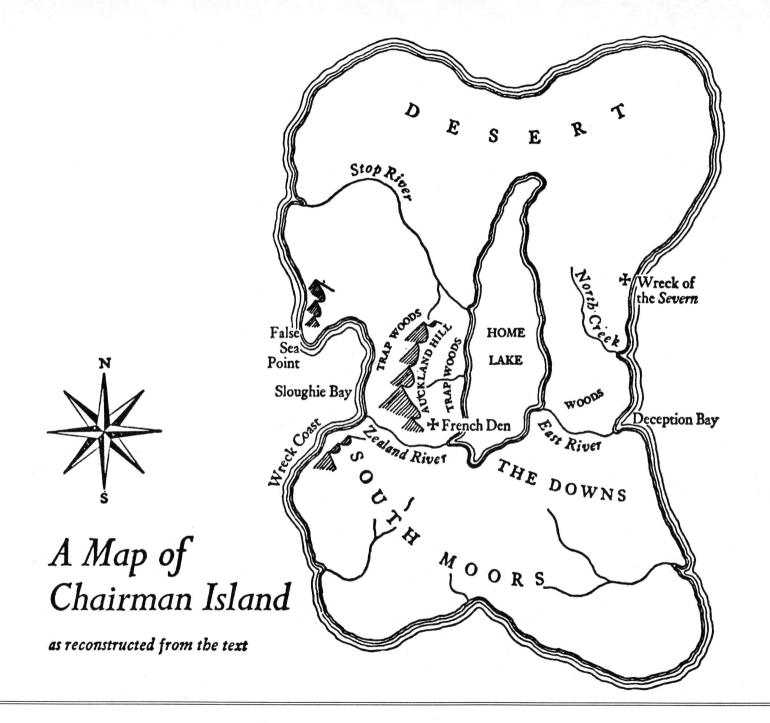

A Map of
Chairman Island

as reconstructed from the text

SEA OF DREAMS

Rudyard Kipling's "The Brushwood Boy" appeared in *Century Magazine* in December 1895. It chronicles the dream journeys of a boy named Georgie. Other dreamlands are charted in better detail, we will note later, and are interesting even if one does not read the story, but this map is tied to the story. Dreamland stories can have a person realizing that he is dreaming. Georgie often knows he is dreaming, and will wade through rivers or burn down cities for his own amusement.

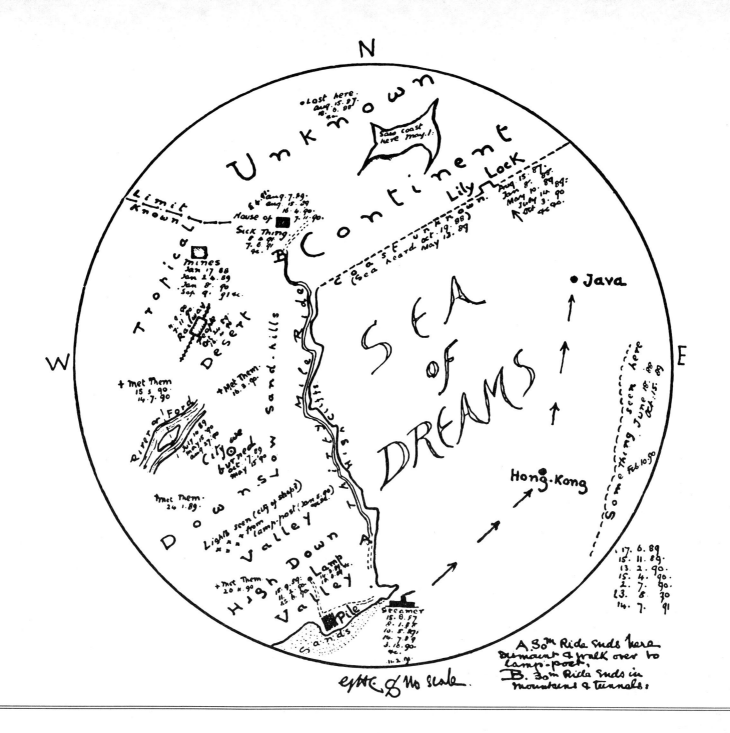

THE INTERIOR WORLD

The hollow Earth story is moderately common in fantastic literature. This map is from William R. Bradshaw's *Goddess of Atvatabar* (New York: Douthitt, 1892). Most of the hollow Earth stories stem from the theory popularized by John Cleves Symmes, though Symmes used a series of concentric spheres. As early as 1820, a fictional account of a hollow Earth was published. For the best general description of hollow Earth theories see Martin Gardner's *Fads and Fallacies in the Name of Science* (New York: Dover, 1957).

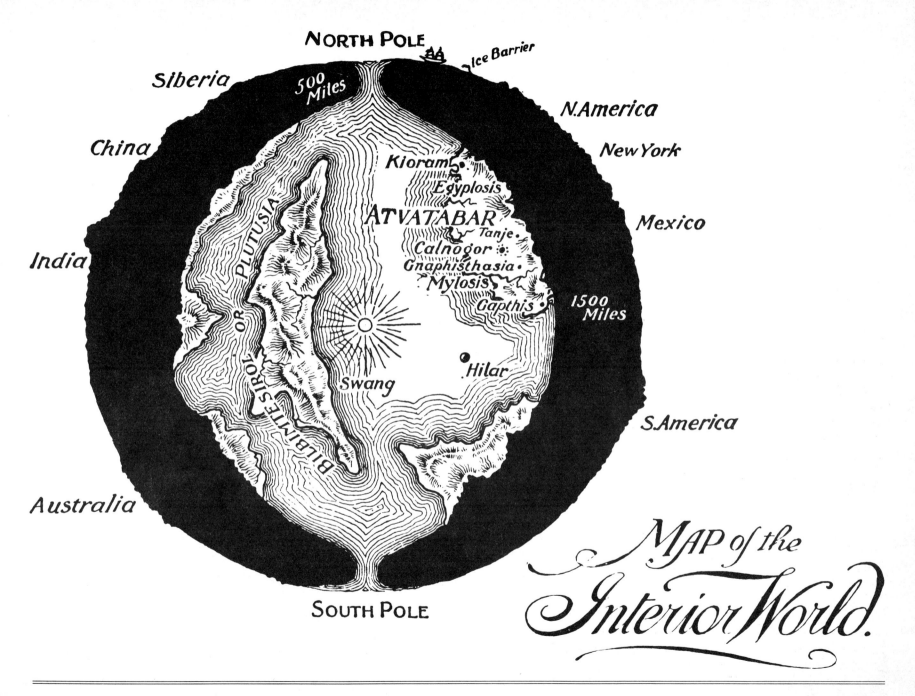

MAP of the Interior World.

OZ AND ENVIRONS

One of the most famous imaginary lands of all time is *Oz*. Created by L. Frank Baum in 1900, the first Oz story, *The Wizard of Oz*, chronicled the adventures of Dorothy, who was transported to Oz from Kansas in a tornado. Subsequent Oz stories, written by Mr. Baum as well as others, filled in the geography of Oz and nearby lands. One problem did arise, however, because Mr. Baum did not observe normal cartographic conventions when drawing the first map of Oz. West was to the right and East was to the left. The original compass rose pointed out the proper directions, but later reprintings "corrected" the compass rose and did not change the map. This was somewhat confusing because the stories would describe a location as being East of another place but on the map it would appear to the West. Current maps of Oz have been corrected to agree with the stories.

While Oz has been mapped by several sources, the best, reproduced here, is by James E. Haff and Dick Martin. Copies in color are available from Fred M. Meyer, International Wizard of Oz Club, Box 95, Kinderhook, Illinois 62345 (two maps and an explanatory leaflet). The history of the cartography of Oz is discussed in the Spring 1963, Autumn 1967, Autumn 1970, and Spring 1972 issues of *The Baum Bugle,* the official journal of the International Wizard of Oz Club.

The
MARVELOUS
LAND of OZ
and
The MAGICAL
COUNTRIES
surrounding OZ

EXPLANATORY
NOTES
by
James E. Haff

Based on the
Original Map
drawn by
Professor
H.M.WOGGLEBUG,T.E.

Revised
in accordance with
the
Royal Histories
of
OZ

Published
by
The International
Wizard of Oz Club
by
Royal Appointment
of
Her Gracious Majesty
OZMA
of OZ

N
W E
S

JAMES
E. HAFF
Delineavit

Revised 1972

DICK
MARTIN
Sculpsit

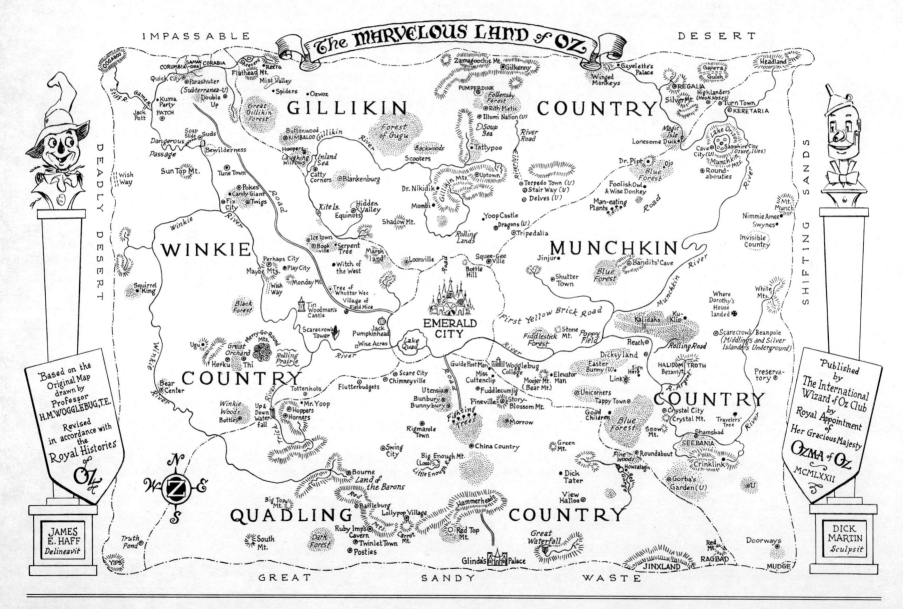

The MARVELOUS Land of OZ

IMPASSABLE   DESERT

DEADLY DESERT

SHIFTING SANDS

GILLIKIN COUNTRY

WINKIE COUNTRY

MUNCHKIN COUNTRY

QUADLING COUNTRY

EMERALD CITY

Based on the Original Map drawn by Professor H.M.WOGGLEBUG, T.E. Revised in accordance with the Royal Histories of OZ

JAMES E. HAFF Delineavit

Published by The International Wizard of Oz Club by Royal Appointment of Her Gracious Majesty OZMA of OZ MCMLXXII

DICK MARTIN Sculpsit

GREAT   SANDY   WASTE

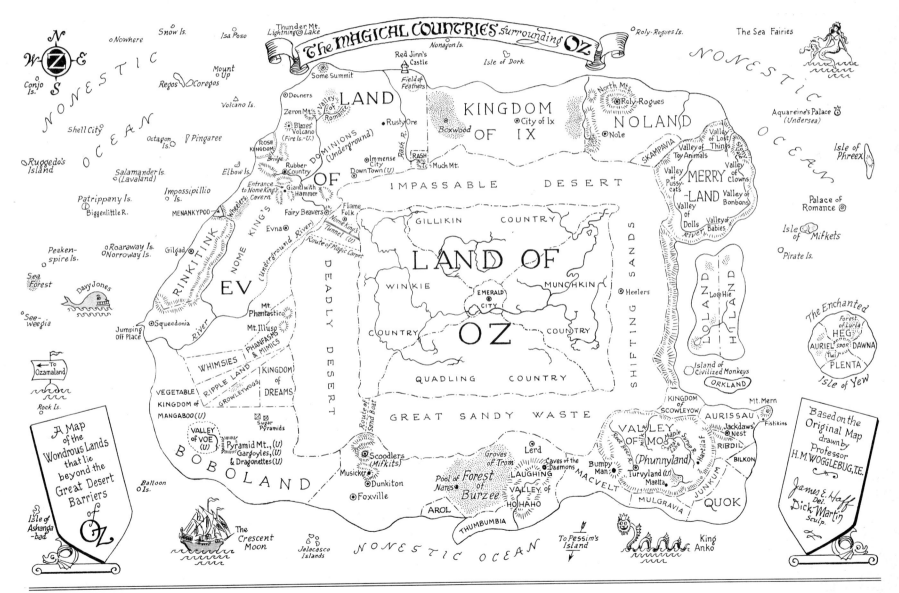

MOUSELAND

Edward Earle Childs' *The Wonders of Mouseland* (New York: Abbey Press, 1901), in which this map appears, is an obvious imitation of Gulliver's trip to Lilliput. Marvin Lampkin is shipwrecked on the Great Barrier Reef but manages to survive. He is captured by a nation of intelligent mice and made a prisoner in the manner of Gulliver. Mouseland, he discovers, was originally settled by shipwrecked mice, but because this pioneer band managed to release a supernatural being from bondage, they were granted human intelligence. Some of the mice become civilized (truly civilized because they have wars!) while others remain barbarians. There is a touch of genteel turn-of-the-century racism in having the ruling class be white mice. Intrepid explorers journey to the lands of man and even splice into a telegraph cable so Mouseland can be kept informed of their affairs.

Knowing their only hope for survival is to go unnoticed by mankind, the mice ponder the fate of Marvin. He is the only shipwrecked man to survive the Great Barrier Reef and, obviously, cannot be permitted to leave. The mouse nation of Halloway, which captured Marvin, makes him a citizen and sets him to performing tasks especially suited to his size. He helps fight a war with Aola, puts down pirates in the Double Isles, helps explore the wilder climes of Mouseland, plant colonies, and a host of other activities which Marvin in his narrative modestly dismisses in a few words. The other mouse nations demand Marvin be internationalized, but Halloway refuses. In the ensuing carnage Marvin manages to escape from Mouseland and is rescued by a passing steamer.

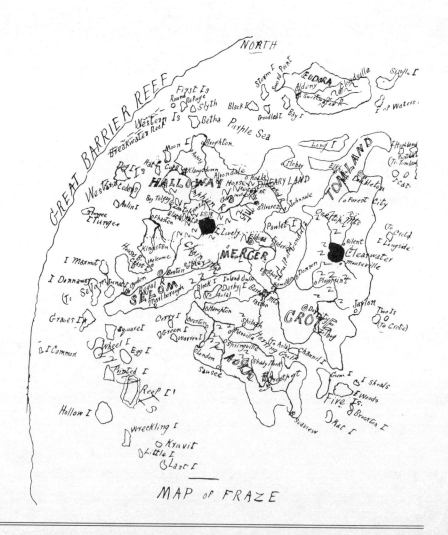

MAP of FRAZE

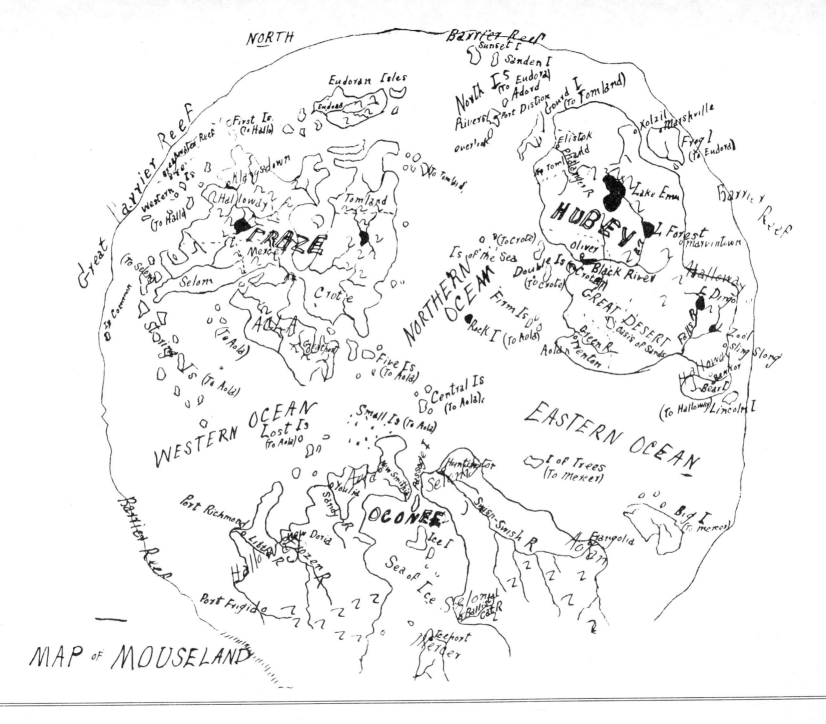

MAP of MOUSELAND

GOSPEL TEMPERANCE RAILROAD MAP

Perhaps under the same management as the "Temperance Rail Road" shown on a previous map, but definitely a different line, is the Gospel Temperance Railroad, Great Celestial Route. It runs quite straight from Decisionville to Celestial City. The scenery looks pretty drab; the route to City of Destruction looks like more fun. One has a choice of routes, crosslines, and side trips; but while it may be fun getting there and a nice place to visit friends, City of Destruction does not look like a place to spend all eternity. The map was drawn in 1908 by G. E. Bula and is reproduced from a copy in the Library of Congress.

GOSPEL TEMPERANCE RAILROAD MAP

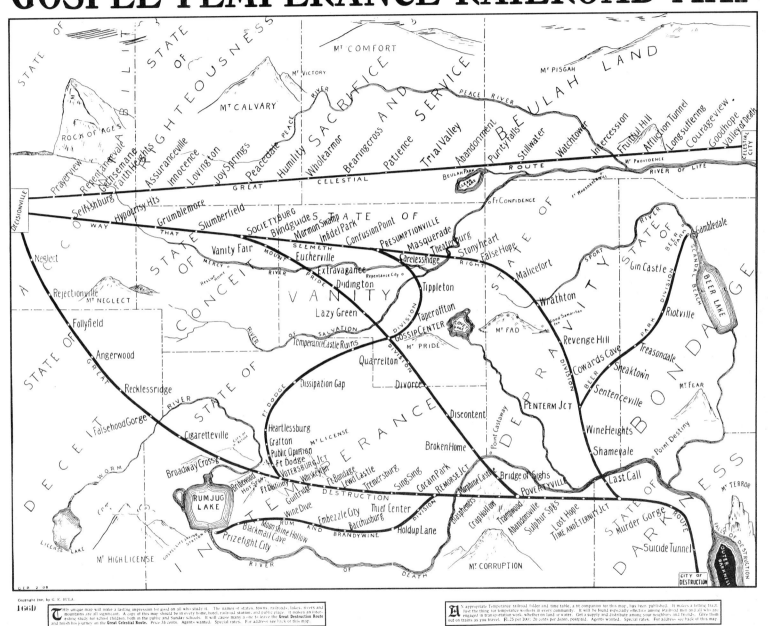

166D

This unique map will make a lasting impression for good on all who study it. The names of states, towns, railroads, lakes, rivers and mountains are all significant. A copy of this map should be in every home, hotel, railroad station, and public place. It makes an interesting study for school children, both in the public and Sunday schools. It will cause many a one to leave the **Great Destruction Route** and finish his journey on the **Great Celestial Route.** Price 35 cents. Agents wanted. Special rates. For address see back of this map.

An appropriate Temperance railroad folder and time table, a fit companion for this map, has been published. It makes a telling tract. Just the thing for temperance workers in every community. It will be found especially effective among Railroad men and all who are engaged in transportation work, whether on land or water. Get a supply and distribute among your neighbors and friends. Give them out on trains as you travel. $1.25 per 100; 20 cents per dozen, postpaid. Agents wanted. Special rates. For address see back of this map.

THE WORLDS OF EDGAR RICE BURROUGHS

Barsoom

Of all the creators of imaginary lands, few match Edgar Rice Burroughs (1875–1950) in quantity of output. Not content with a mere four or five, he created a new land with almost every story, or at least some further elaboration of an earlier described one. Indeed, it is the creation of whole worlds that is the real secret of the appeal of Burroughs. We know the slave girl will turn out to be a princess (or at least noble born) at the end and the hero will win her, but the countryside through which they romp and fight is infinitely varied. At the least there is usually a lost city, and for those stories set upon Earth, a lost race. Alas, the modern mapping of Africa has forever banished Opar, the City of Gold, the Lost Empire, Pal-ul-Don, and other spots visited by Tarzan.

Barsoom, as Burroughs called Mars, was essentially a desert world. The canals were dug by the dominant Red race and most of their civilization was along the canals. The deserts were dominated by giant four armed Green Men. Hidden remnants of the Yellow race were at the North Pole while the White and Black races were at the Southern Pole. The Rift had a colony of Blacks, and a small settlement of Whites were in Horz, a ruined city. Ancient cities dotted the desert, abandoned with the drying of the oceans. The Toonolian Marshes are the largest wet land on the surface, being all that is left of a once great ocean. Phundahl is a barbaric kingdom steeped in superstition, and Toonol is an advanced scientific state. The empire based at the twin cities of Helium is the nation with which the Earth adventurer John Carter casts his lot.

With one exception ("Wild Island"), the following maps were drawn by Mr. Burroughs. Two works that give extensive background material on Barsoom are Richard Lupoff's *Barsoom: Edgar Rice Burroughs and the Martian Vision* (Baltimore, Md.: Mirage Press, 1976) and John Flint Roy's *A Guide to Barsoom* (New York: Ballantine Books, 1976).

Map of one of the hemispheres of BARSOOM. © 1973 by Edgar Rice Burroughs, Inc.
Map drawn by Edgar Rice Burroughs.

Map of other hemisphere of BARSOOM. © 1973 by Edgar Rice Burroughs, Inc.
Drawn by Edgar Rice Burroughs.

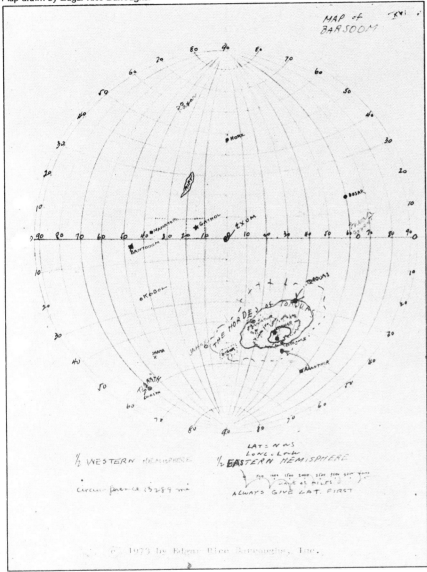

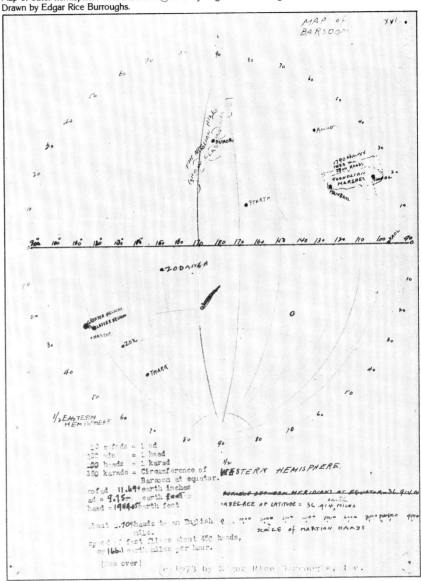

Pal-ul-Don

Somewhere in the present Republic of Zaire surrounded by an
impassable morass—well, almost impassable—is the land of
Pal-ul-Don. Jane, in the previous book, was kidnapped by Germans
and Tarzan seeks his mate with vengence. Pal-ul-Don is a primitive
land with giant lizards still roaming the countryside and a
subhuman civilization being built by Pithecanthropi. Tarzan
finds Jane, and the entire Tarzan family, for Korak, the son of
Tarzan, following his father, are declared gods by the "people"
of Pal-ul-Don.

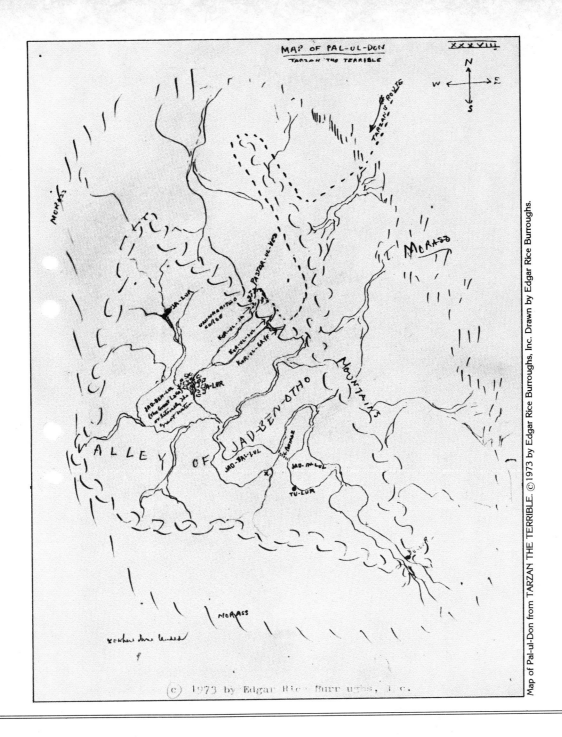

Land of
the Ant Men

Burroughs' Africa is just full of impassable barriers. Behind a thorn
forest is the land of the Ant Men. These humanoids stand about a
foot high. Tarzan is flying overhead and is forced to bail out.
Captured by the Ant Men, he is reduced to their stature by one of
their scientists. After many adventures he manages to pass the
impassable thorn forest in his shortened condition and springs to
full size when the treatment wears off.

In most of his lost lands, Burroughs gives us a language, and
in many we are treated to a written tongue as well. The worlds of
Burroughs are never simple; they always suppose a total ecology
even if it always is not spelled out. From the mute anthropoid
Alali living in caves, to the huge domed cities of the Ant men,
it all ties together.

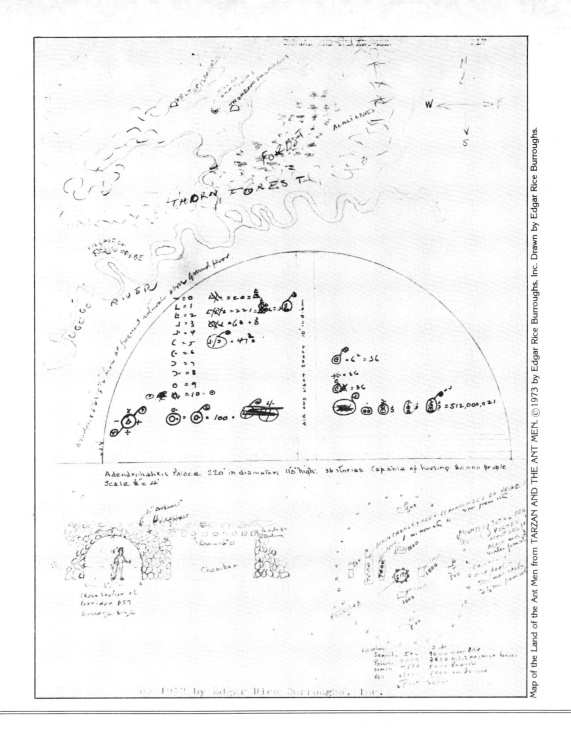

Onthar
and Thenar

In both *Tarzan and the City of Gold* and *Tarzan the Magnificent,*
Tarzan journeys to the lands of Onthar and Thenar. The Ontharians
worship lions and adorn their city with gold while the Thenarians
worship elephants and use ivory. The lost race in this case seems
to be Greek (ancient, of course). The two cities are constantly at
war, and here we have a favorite theme of Burroughs in many of
his stories: two cities at war from time immemorial. It should be
noted that the nobles of the two cities fight. When a revolution
drives the Athnean nobility out of Athne, the Ontharian nobles from
Cathne help put down the revolt and restore the old order so they
will have enemies worth fighting. Burroughs was more of a social
satirist than many realize.

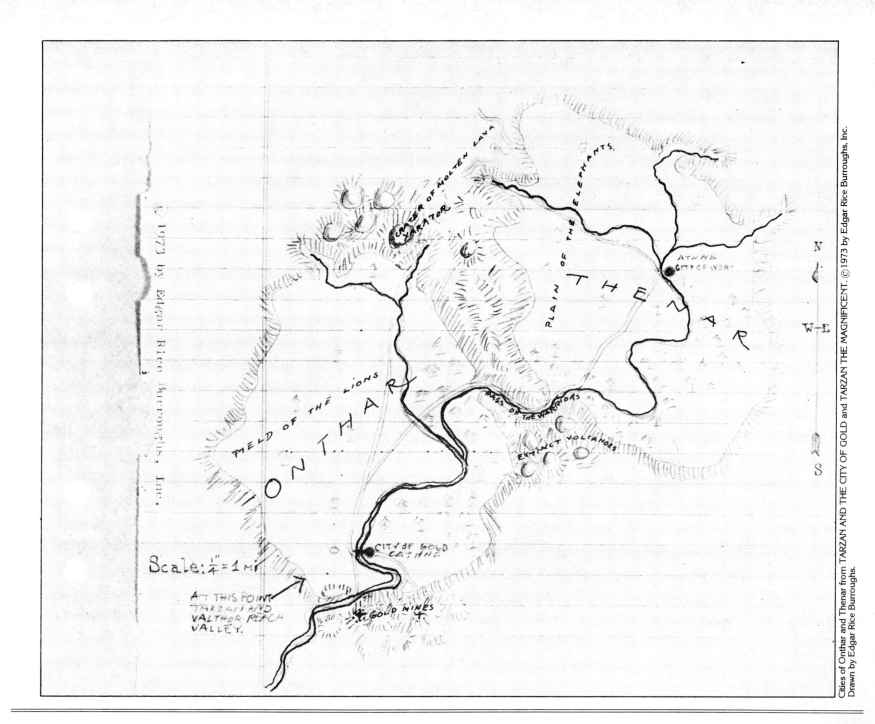

Cities of Onthar and Thenar from TARZAN AND THE CITY OF GOLD and TARZAN THE MAGNIFICENT. © 1973 by Edgar Rice Burroughs, Inc. Drawn by Edgar Rice Burroughs.

The Lost Empire

Here Tarzan finds an isolated outpost of Ancient Rome still carrying out the old traditions. The two cities at war are Castra Sanguinarius and Castrum Marinus. At this point one is tempted to say: "All these lost races look alike." Not so, though superficially it may seem so. The lost races and cities always have special touches that make them different. After the first few stories, one begins to read Burroughs more for the faraway places with strange sounding names rather than for the adventures of the lead character.

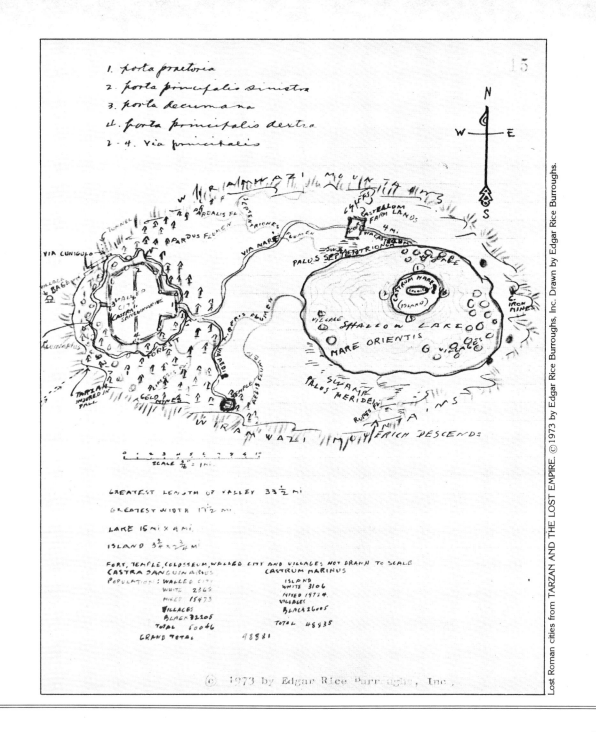

Amtor (Venus)

This map is the endpaper design for Burroughs' Venus series. These books concern the adventures of Carson Napier whose rocket ship has crashed on Venus. What makes this map so interesting is that it depicts Venus not as Burroughs conceives it but as his Venerians conceive it. In the Southern hemisphere the belief is that the world has for its center a great lake of fire while the edge of the world is a wall of ice. The world is, of course, thought to be flat. Map makers must conform to the religious cosmology. The map is obviously distorted since the outer circle is the South Pole or close to it while the center of the map is the equator.

The most interesting feature on the map is the Amtorian script. It is worth mentioning that the city of Kooaad on the island of Vepaja is carved out of the upper level of living trees. Havatoo is a city of super scientists turned inward on themselves to the point of ignoring the city of Kormor just across the river where a renegade scientist is setting up a nation of zombies. The Venus series began late in Burroughs' life, and he never developed Amtor the way he did Barsoom.

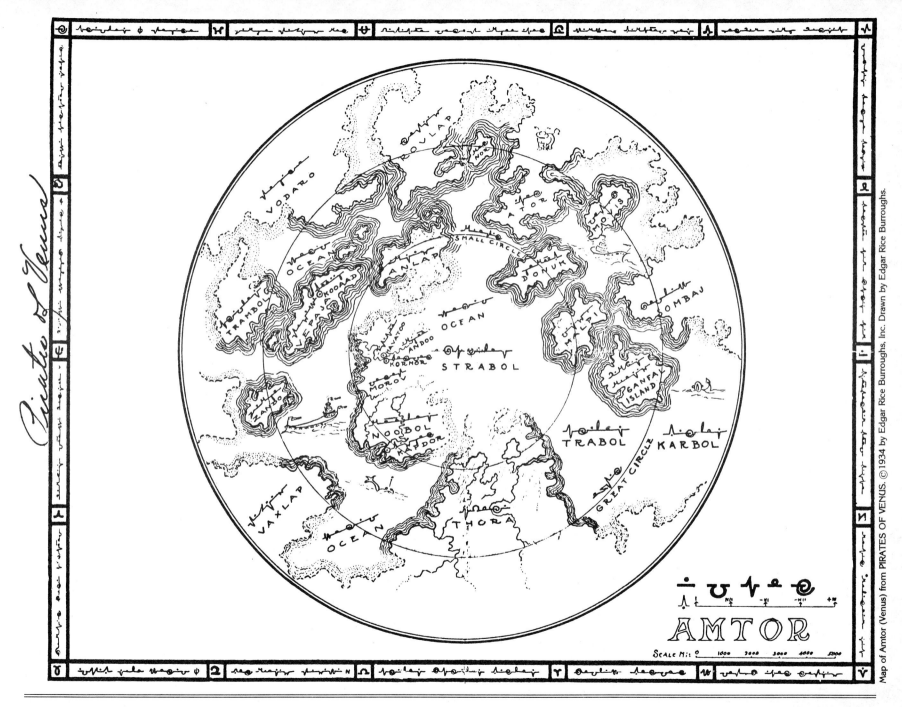

AMTOR

SCALE MI: 0   1000   2000   3000   4000   5000

Pellucidar

Abner Perry is the unluckiest of inventors—his inventions do not work the way he wants. He and David Innes set off in a mechanical mole to prospect for mineral wealth but discover the mole can not be turned. They drill down to a hollow Earth. The hollow Earth is a rather common device in popular literature but, as usual, Burroughs has furnished his more lavishly than most others. The humans are at about stone age development—at least in the area in which David and Abner emerge. A race of female flying reptiles, the Mahars, has developed a civilization of sorts but it is in decline. The land of Awful Shadow is caused by a small planetoid or moonlet hovering over the same spot and shutting out the rays of the central sun which everywhere else gives a perpetual noon. David organizes the humans against the tyranny of the Mahars and their ape-men allies, with Abner providing the military technology—gunpowder. David drives the Mahars out of his immediate neighborhood and is proclaimed Emperor of Pellucidar.

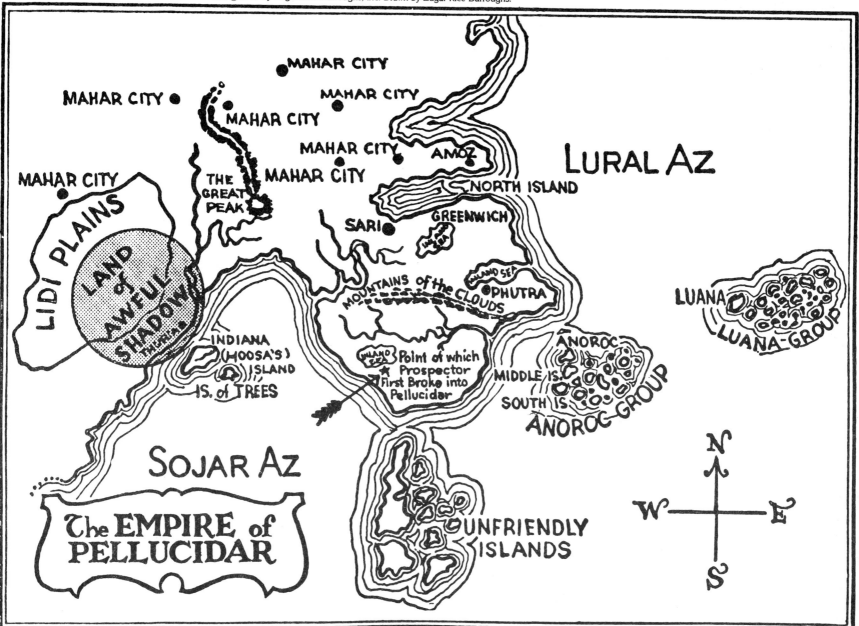

The Moon

Many critics consider *The Moon Maid* to be Burroughs' best work. It is in three related but independent parts. A space faring vessel from Earth crashes not on the Moon but in the Moon, plunging through a crater to a hollow center. Air and water are on the inner surface. A renegade Earthman leads the Lunar hordes to conquest of Earth. Generations later the Earthmen throw off the alien yoke. All we need note here is a repetition of the hollow world theme.

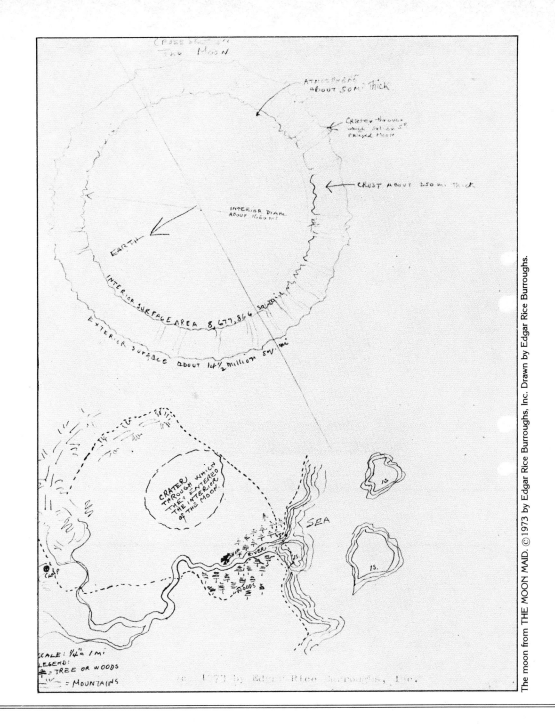

The moon from THE MOON MAID. © 1973 by Edgar Rice Burroughs, Inc. Drawn by Edgar Rice Burroughs.

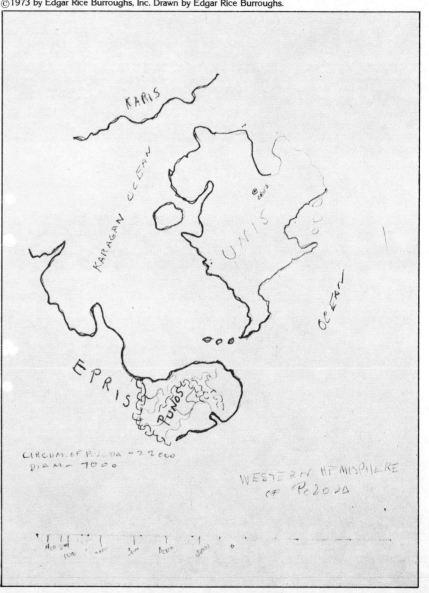

Poloda and Omos

Not content with mere worlds, Edgar Rice Burroughs created a whole solar system. The eleven planets share the same impossible orbit around the star Omos. Burroughs also has an atmosphere belt between the various worlds. Part of Poloda, scene of most of the action, is shown in more detail. As always, empires and ecologies are worked out.

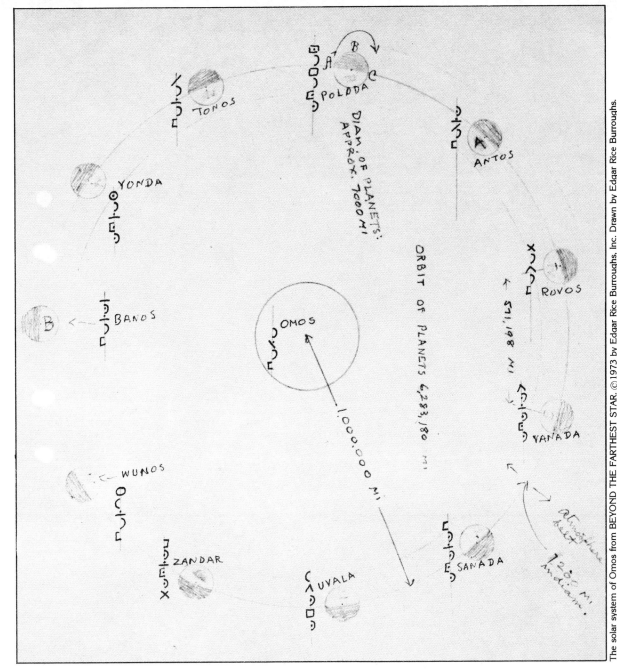

Caspak
and Caprona

Hidden away in the wastes of the South Pacific is the island of
Caprona. The inevitable dinosaurs and ape-men appear but
Burroughs outdid himself in creating the biology of this land:
everything evolves. This means that small lizards become dinosaurs
while individual lemuroids change to pithecoids and then to
humans—and beyond. The next step beyond mankind is the
winged Weiroos, skulking on their island stronghold very bitter
about the outcome because no women have evolved into Weiroos.
Into this world stumble victims of a World War I submarine attack.
Setting themselves in for a long seige, they build Fort Dinosaur and
keep sending messages in bottles, hoping for rescue. After many
adventures it comes.

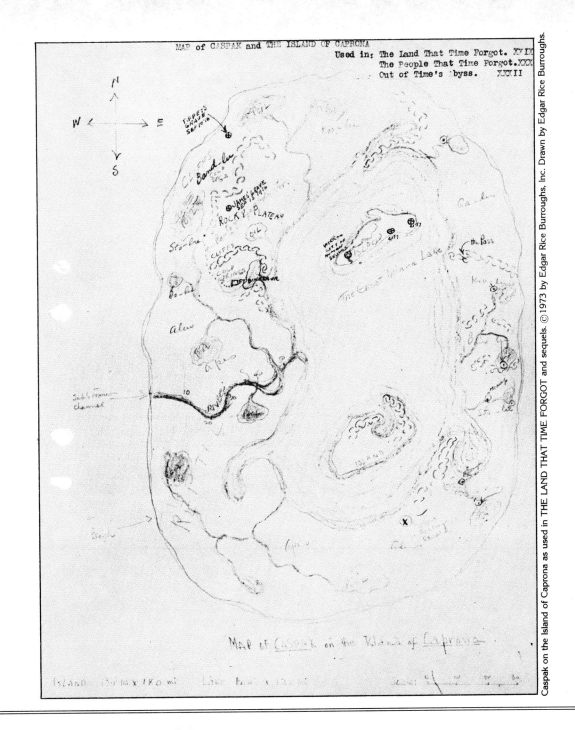

Wild Island

Puny Waldo Emerson Smith-Jones of Boston is washed ashore on a lonely Pacific island where the inhabitants are still in the stone age. He manages to survive, becoming muscular in the process. Nadara, the cave girl, turns out to be the child of a French count and countess shipwrecked years before.

While the story and map are not that interesting in themselves, even to devotees of Burroughs, the map is part of a series of maps which appeared on the back covers of many Dell paperbacks in the early 1940s. Later we'll show another one. These maps illustrated the locale of the novel or a story in the collection.

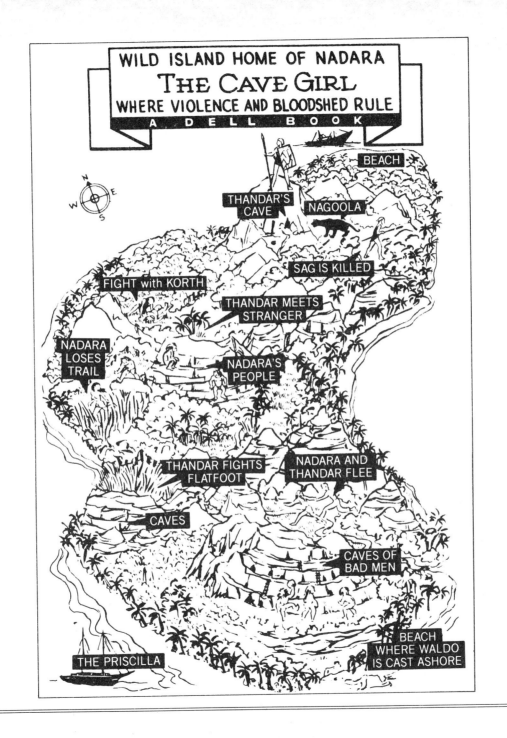

POOH'S TURF

The misadventures of Pooh Bear is standard fare for younger readers. My own favorite episode is that "In Which Pooh and Piglet Go Hunting and Nearly Catch a Woozle." Pooh finding the North Pole is also of interest to the geographically inclined. This map, or view, is from the book *Winnie-the-Pooh* by A. A. Milne (New York: E. P. Dutton, 1926). Decorations by E. H. Shepard.

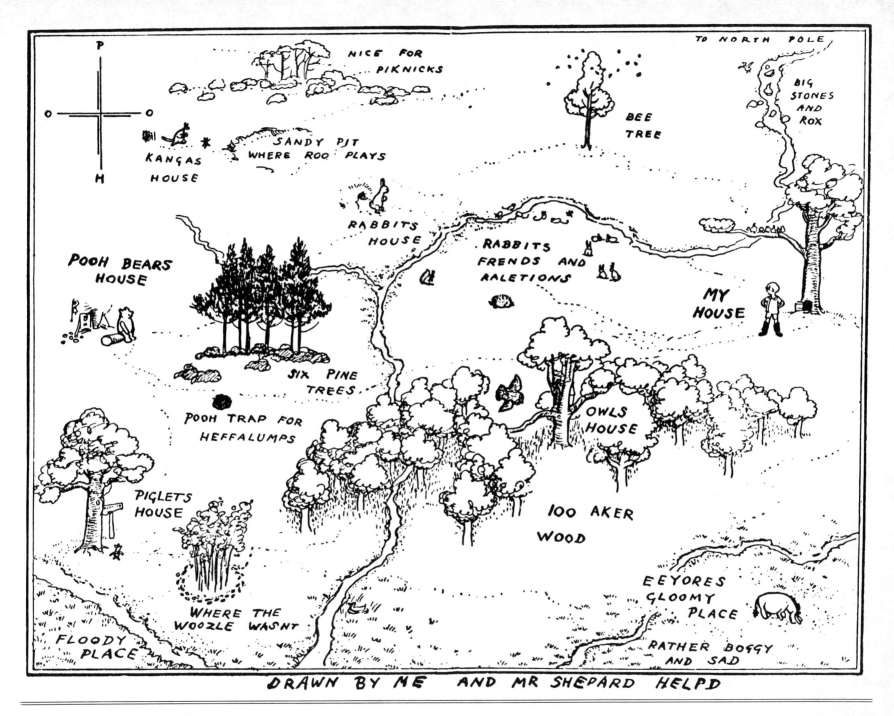

POOH
O ← → O
H

TO NORTH POLE

NICE FOR
PIKNICKS

BEE
TREE

BIG
STONES
AND
ROX

KANGAS
HOUSE

SANDY PIT
WHERE ROO PLAYS

RABBITS
HOUSE

RABBITS
FRENDS AND
RALETIONS

MY
HOUSE

POOH BEARS
HOUSE

SIX PINE
TREES

OWLS
HOUSE

POOH TRAP FOR
HEFFALUMPS

PIGLETS
HOUSE

100 AKER
WOOD

EEYORES
GLOOMY
PLACE

WHERE THE
WOOZLE WASNT

FLOODY
PLACE

RATHER BOGGY
AND SAD

DRAWN BY ME   AND MR SHEPARD HELPD

POICTESME

In these latter days the works of James Branch Cabell are enjoying
a well deserved revival, and much of the credit for this goes to the
adult fantasy series published by Ballantine as Del Rey Books.
While the action of Mr. Cabell's rollickingly hilarious (and
magnificently written) stories is set in many places—Jurgen, for
instance, travels to Heaven and ascends the Throne of God—the
Earthly focus is the land of Poictesme. Poictesme is vaguely located
in southern France during the Middle Ages. It bears about the same
relation to Provence as Arkham does to Salem in the works of H. P.
Lovecraft. For many years this map, drawn by Peter Koch is 1928,
was (and for some of us it still is) the standard map of Poictesme.
Recently *Kalki*, the journal of Cabell Scholarship, published a
topographic map by Judith Blish in Volume 2, page 87.

POICTESME

Published By Argus Books—Chicago. © 1929

HYBORIAN AGE

The genre of heroic fantasy goes back to the oral tradition of the
Germanic tribes—at least that far back. Between then and now the
story of the heroic and mighty hero has wandered about in folk
tales, fairy tales, mythology, and general literature. In its latest form,
the "sword-and-sorcery" tale, heroic fantasy, is enjoying a revival in
the United States. Foremost among the host of mighty-thewed
barbarians is Conan the Cimmerian, created by Robert E. Howard
(1906–1936). The stage for his wanderings from birth in the frozen
North to the throne of Aquilonia is the Hyborian Age, a time
between the sinking of Atlantis and the dawn of modern history.
Howard could somehow make the reader believe for a while the
fantastic civilizations of this lost time. An entire history of the period
was worked out, several non-Conan stories being set before and
after Conan's time in the history. This is not the place to list
minutely all the inconsistencies in the stories, but I should mention
that for all the faults of the stories by Robert E. Howard, they are
quite readable and entertaining—in the last analysis the best
reasons for reading fiction.

  This map was drawn by David Kyle and was used as the
endpaper design in the Gnome Press editions of the Conan books,
published between 1950 and 1955. With the increasing popularity
of Conan, there have been several different versions of the map
published more recently: Marvel Comics did one, George Barr did
one in color, both Tim Conrad and Julian May Dikty drew maps
showing more of the world of Conan than Kyle's map does, and
Howard's own crude sketch has been reproduced in critical studies
of him. The Hyborian Age has won a respected place for itself
among other popular, imaginary lands.

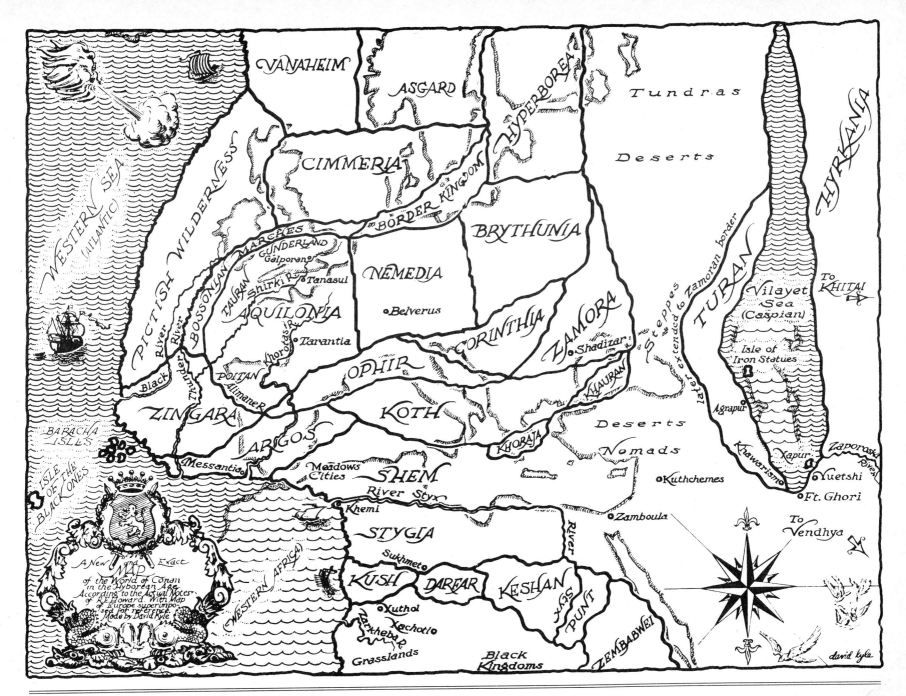

VANAHEIM

ASGARD

HYPERBOREA

Tundras

Deserts

WESTERN SEA (ATLANTIC)

PICTISH WILDERNESS

CIMMERIA

BORDER KINGDOM

BRYTHUNIA

HYRKANIA

MARCHES

GUNDERLAND

Galporan

Thunder River

Bossonian

Tauran

Shirki R.

Tanasul

NEMEDIA

Belverus

TURAN

Vilayet Sea (Caspian)

To KHITAI

Steppes

later extended to Zamoran border

Black River

AQUILONIA

Khoras R.

Tarantia

CORINTHIA

ZAMORA

Shadizar

Isle of Iron Statues

POITAN

Alimane R.

OPHIR

ZINGARA

KOTH

KIAURAN

Agrapur

Deserts

BARACHA ISLES

ARGOS

Messantia

Meadows Cities

SHEM

Khoraja

Nomads

Khawarismo

Xapur

Zaporoska River

Yuetshi

ISLE OF THE BLACK ONES

River Styx

Kuthchemes

Ft. Ghori

Khemi

STYGIA

Zamboula

To Vendhya

A New and Exact MAP of the World of Conan in the Hyborean Age According to the Actual Notes of R.E. Howard With Map of Europe superimposed for reference. Made by David Kyle

Sukhmet

KUSH

DARFAR

KESHAN

River Styx

PUNT

WESTERN AFRICA

Xuthol

Xuchotlo

Zarkheba R.

Grasslands

Black Kingdoms

ZEMBABWEI

david kyle

ALIMENTARY CANAL

George S. Chappell was a humorist of the 1920s and 1930s. He may have been forgotten by the general public but he has left a phrase in the language: the title of his most memorable book. *Through the Alimentary Canal with Gun and Camera* (New York: Stokes, 1930) is the sort of book few of my generation have read but of which many have heard. The title was supposed to have been originated by Robert Benchley as a talk, but George Chappell expanded on the title and produced a funny book. It's a parody of the popular adventure narrative. Four intrepid explorers set off to chart the Alimentary Canal and its tributaries. On the map you will note the Bile River being formed at the conjunction of Gall River and Spleen River. One whole chapter is devoted to "The Sources of the Bile." Allow me to quote briefly from the book to give you the flavor: entering the oral cavity, Chappell notes: "The Molars show unmistakable signs of having belonged to our earliest rock formations, although some dental barriers closely resemble the Great Wall of China, which was erected shortly after the second Tartar Invasion." The human innards are treated as an unexplored country.

The map, as well as twelve illustrations in the book, is the work of O. Soglow, a cartoonist better known for the syndicated feature "The Little King" but whose work appears in surprising places.

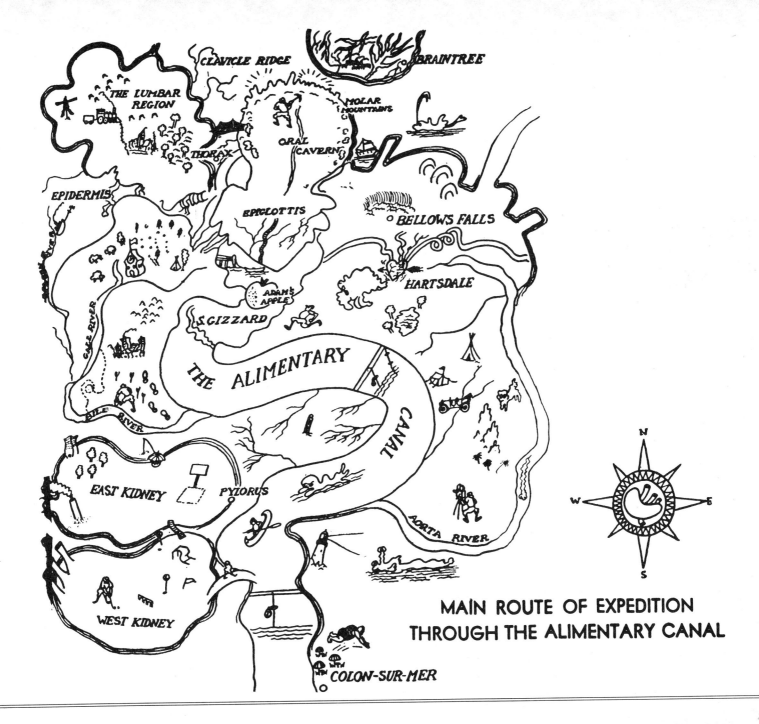

MAIN ROUTE OF EXPEDITION
THROUGH THE ALIMENTARY CANAL

ENVIRONS OF TOAD HALL

The line between a map and a view is a very fine one, if it exists at all. Traditionally a map is more graphic and symbolic while the view is what the country "really" looks like. Even before the rise of aerial photography, the "panoramic view" of a city was quite popular. Since it was then an artist's rendering, all the ugliness could be conveniently disguised.

This decorative view—Ernest H. Shepard's map of Toad Hall from *The Wind in the Willows* by Kenneth Grahame (New York: Charles Scribner's Sons, 1933)—may not be strictly a map but this is my atlas so I am including it.

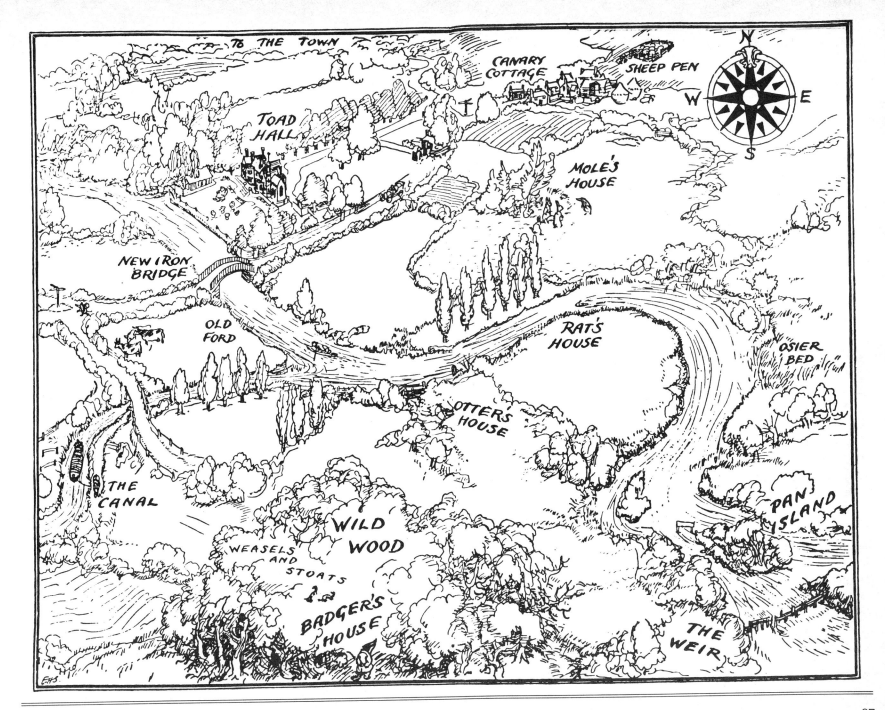

THE WORLDS OF J.R.R. TOLKIEN

The most recent of imagined lands to strike the popular fancy is Middle-earth. Created by J. R. R. Tolkien, it is more than a mere stage for the actions of the Fellowship of the Ring as the Fellowship journeys to Mt. Doom to destroy the One Ring and bring to an end the dominion of Sauron. Middle-earth is a complete world with history, geography, custom, and folklore all interacting.

Cartographically, Middle-earth is more interesting than any other map in this book. Not in what is depicted but in the way it is depicted. The maps on the next few pages are the basic ones from the books: Middle-earth itself tipped into the first two volumes of *Lord of the Rings* (New York: Ballantine Books, 1965); a closer view of Gondor and Mordor in the last volume; Thror's Map and the map of Wilderland from *The Hobbit* (New York: Ballantine Books, 1965). The first volume of *Lord of the Rings* also has a more detailed map of the Shire, home of the Hobbits.

Mirkwood, the large forest shown on one of the upcoming maps, was once called "Greenwood" until a curse descended upon it. Much of Middle-earth was more bountiful in earlier times (the maps date from the Third Age). Note that South Gondor is "now a debatable and desert land." Mordor has been laid waste by volcanic activity.

While these maps are the basic ones, different versions of Middle-earth have been published. All are based on maps in the books but each embellishes a bit. I am unable to give any information about the "black light" version or the one showing landforms. Ballantine Books has published two poster versions: an earlier one by "Brem" (who is Barbara Remington), and a recent one by Pauline Baynes that is probably the more attractive of the two. M. Blackburn has drawn a larger and more detailed map than the original which was published by Peter Bruin. More, no doubt, will make their appearance over the years. I'm waiting for ethnic and linguistic maps of Middle-earth.

Many admirers of Middle-earth stories have gone on to create their own worlds on paper. Stylistically many of these unpublished maps (that it has been my good fortune to see) are derived from the Tolkien map. *The Harvard Lampoon* parody, *Bored of the Rings* (New York: Signet, 1969), has a map which is mildly amusing.

From the long-awaited and recently published *Silmarillion* (New York: Ballantine Books, 1979) we have a map of Beleriand, with neighboring realms, drawn by Christopher Tolkien. The map shows Middle-earth well before the Third Age, a time of Elves contesting with Morgoth. Another source of maps of Middle-earth is J. E. A. Tyler's *The Tolkien Companion* (New York: Avon, 1977) which has maps of Gondor in its prime and decline as well as interesting battle plans.

A MAP OF
MIDDLE-EARTH

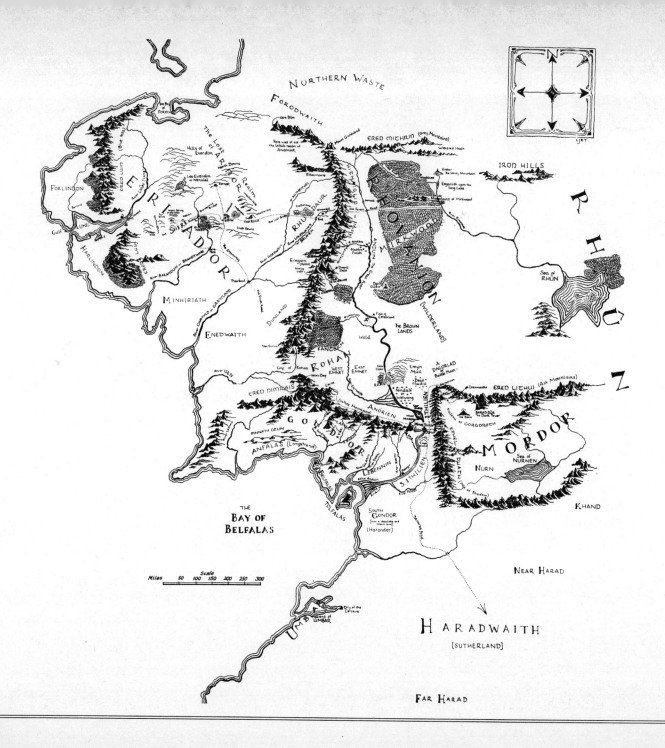

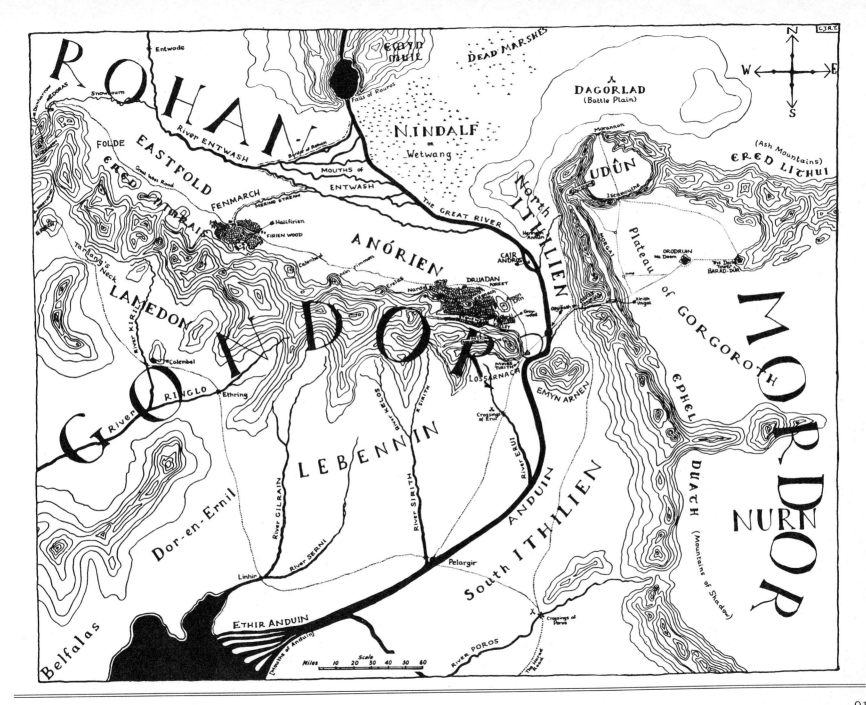

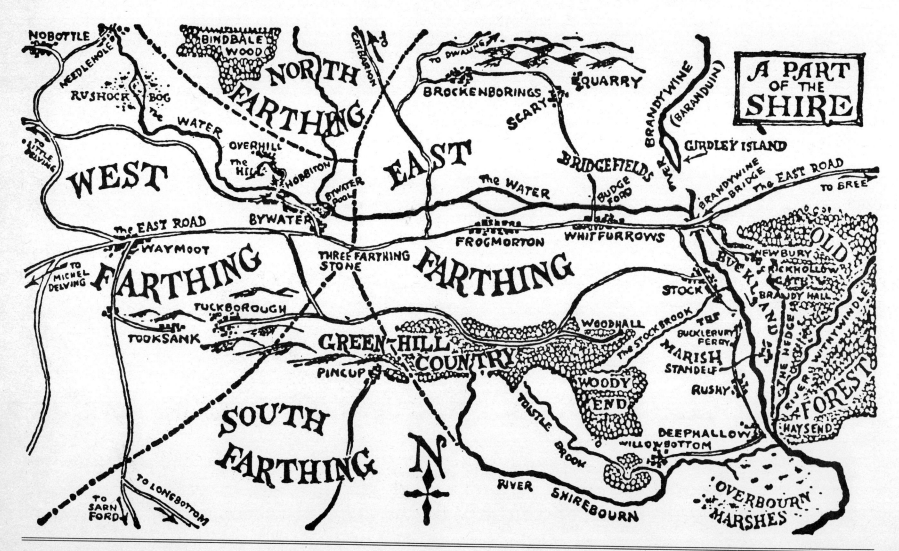

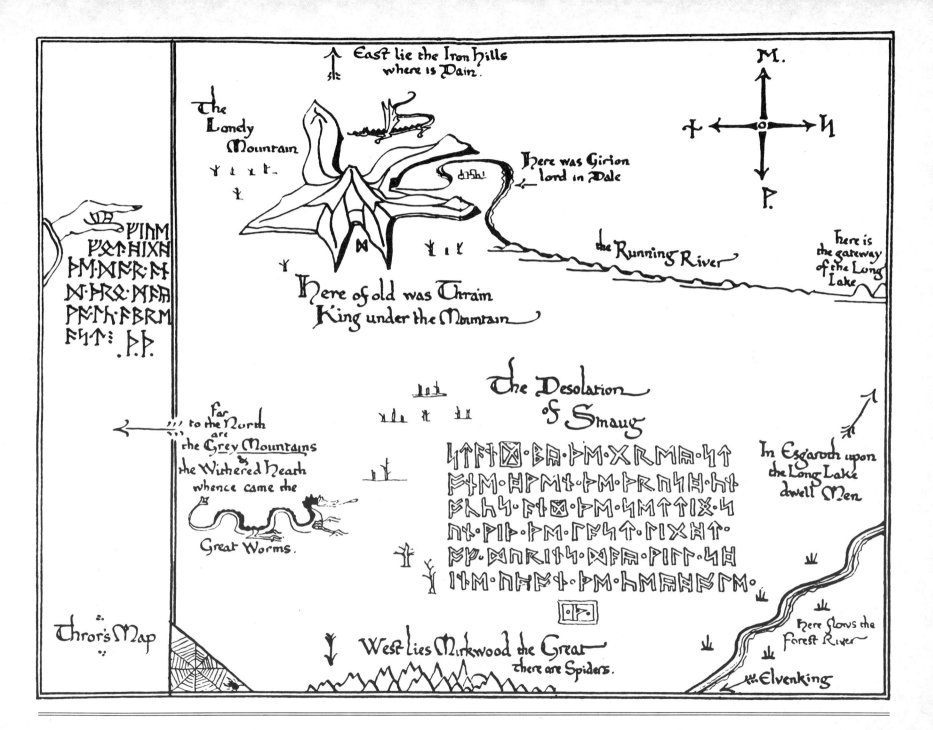

East lie the Iron Hills
where is Dain.

The Lonely Mountain

Here was Girion
lord in Dale

the Running River

here is
the gateway
of the Long
Lake

Here of old was Thrain
King under the Mountain

The Desolation
of Smaug

Far
to the North
are
the Grey Mountains
&
the Withered Heath
whence came the

Great Worms.

In Esgaroth upon
the Long Lake
dwell Men

Thror's Map

West lies Mirkwood the Great
there are Spiders.

Here flows the
Forest River

Elvenking

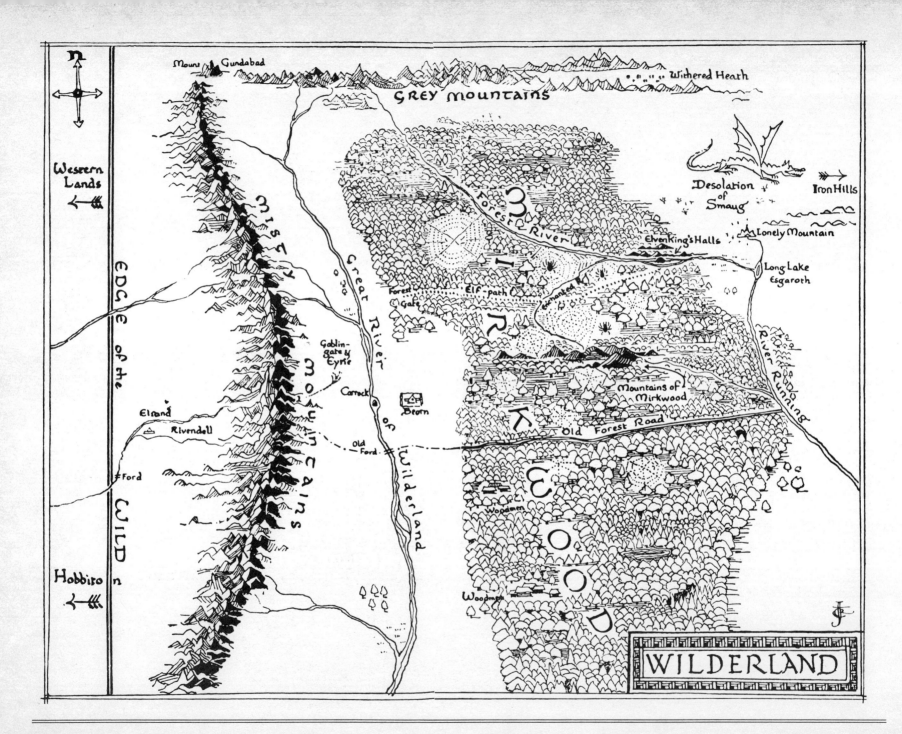

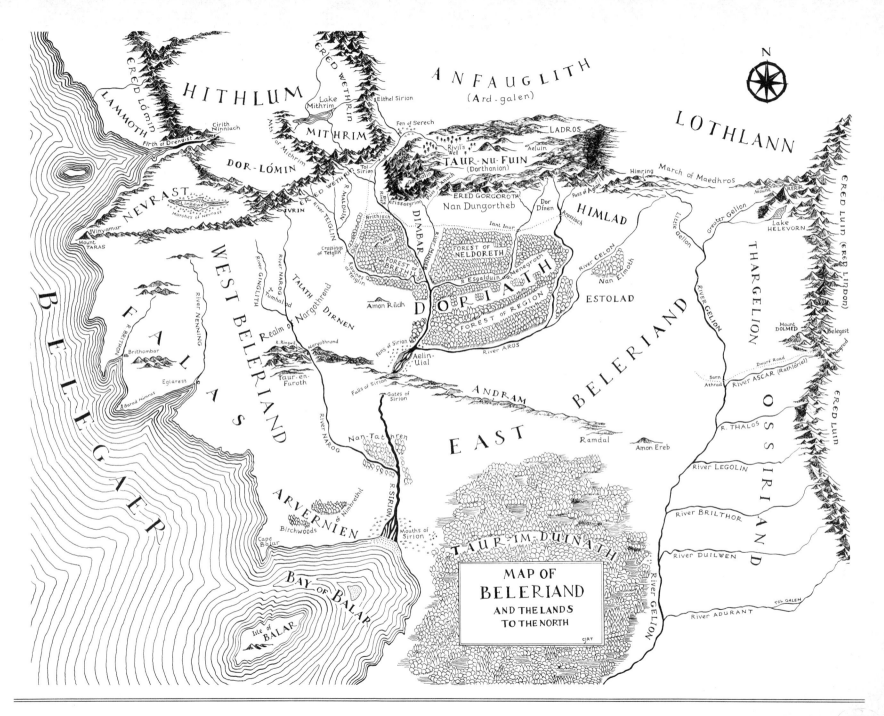

MAP OF
BELERIAND
AND THE LANDS
TO THE NORTH

THE THREE KINGDOMS AND OUROBOROS COUNTRY

The best known works of E. R. Eddison are *Mistress of Mistresses* and *The Worm Ouroboros.* Both of these are grandly wrought fantasies of other worlds. The maps of the Three Kingdoms depict the action (note the troop movements and battle sites) in *Mistress of Mistresses* (New York: E. P. Dutton, 1935). The map for *The Worm Ouroboros* (New York: E. P. Dutton, 1926) first appeared in *Twilight Zine* No. 4, and is the work of Bernard Morris. These are the sort of maps to have in hand while reading the books (along with a cast of characters). It is worth noting one place in Demonland which is rather famous: Owlswick "the place from which the troops did not come."

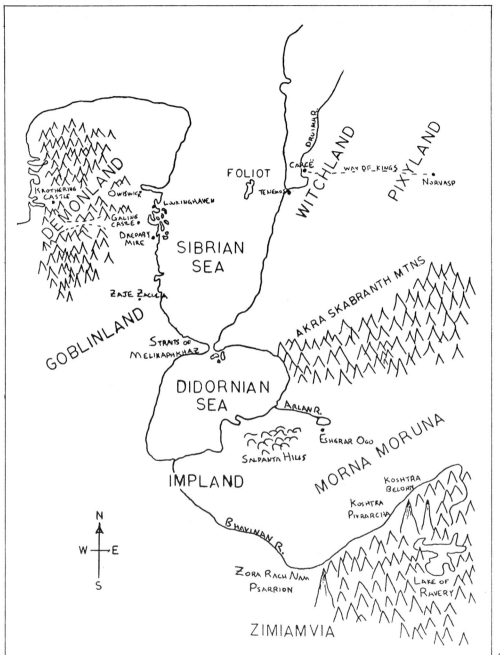

Ouroboros Country

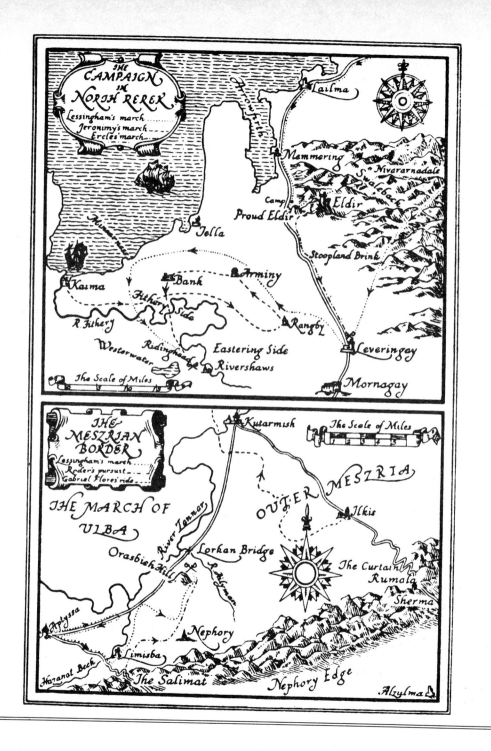

FAIRYLAND

The realm of Faerie is a strange shadow land, lying, according to some, just over the edge of the world, beyond the fields we know, in the border marches of Chaos. The land has been mapped many times but with an impertinence it shares with its inhabitants, never seems to be the same twice. The maps have traditionally been more views than maps, each artist rendering the geography of Fairyland to suit himself, only fair because there is no accepted lay of the land.

Bernard Sleigh's *Anciente Mappe of Fairyland* (London: Sidgwick & Jackson, n. d.) is lavish and attractive. Mr. Sleigh has incorporated mythology, folklore, legends, and literature into his version of Fairyland to produce a monumental view.

AN ANCIENT MAPPE of FAIRY LAND
newly discovered and set forth.

SWALLOWS AND AMAZONS

Helene Carter's map is from Arthur Ransome's *Swallows and Amazons* (Philadelphia: Lippincott, 1941), a story of children playing at seafaring. Small sailboats become galleons, and islets become mysterious islands. Though based on a lake in England's Lake District, which Ransome knew as a child, the map of the area has been drawn as it would have been seen by the Walker children staying at Holly Howe for a summer vacation.

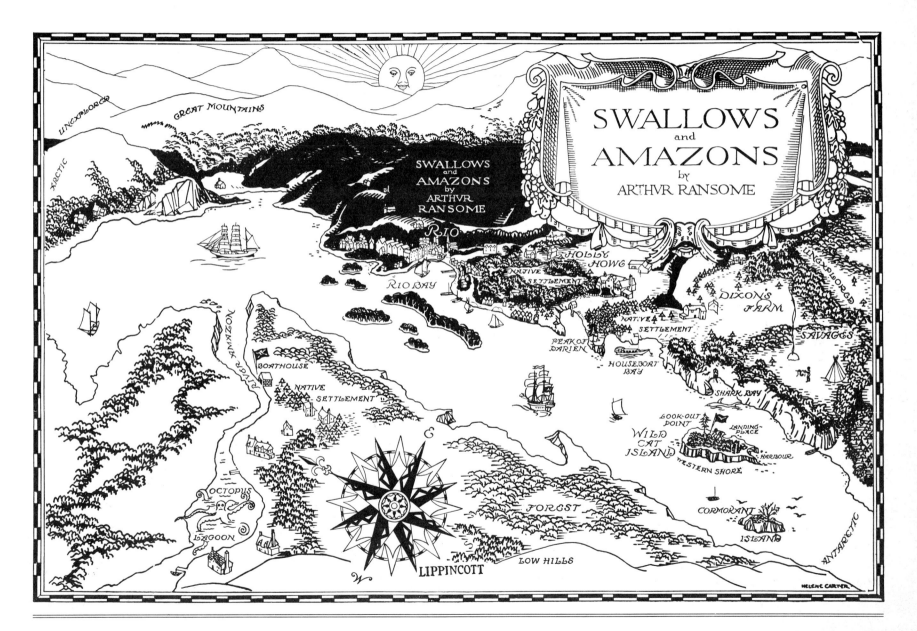

ISLANDIA

Austin Wright's Islandia isn't a utopia. It is a carefully constructed imaginary land with its own history, neither better nor worse than the real world. Wright was a professor of law at the University of California who wrote *Islandia* as a hobby. As well as the novel, he created a complete history and geography for the continent of Karain. *Islandia* inspired a modern sequel, Mark Saxton's *The Islar* (Boston: Houghton Mifflin, 1969). The best study of the subject is *An Introduction to Islandia: its history, customs, laws, language, and geography as prepared by Basil Davenport* (New York: Farrar & Rinehart, 1942).

There are maps both in *Islandia* itself and in Basil Davenport's study, but, as they are difficult to read and even more difficult to reproduce, we offer the map from *The Islar*.

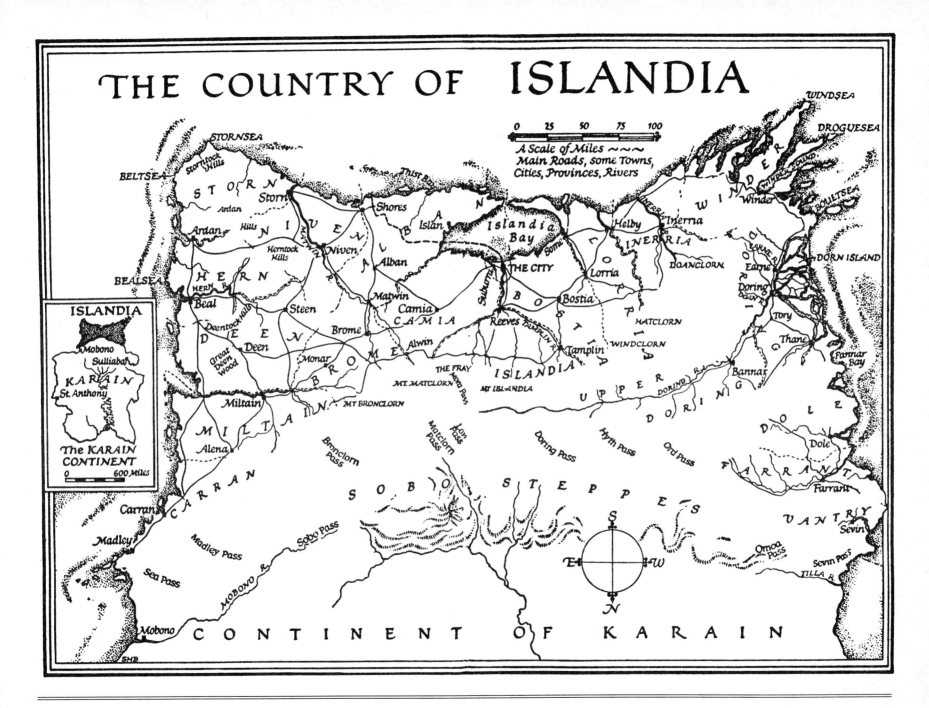

THE COUNTRY OF ISLANDIA

RAINTREE COUNTY

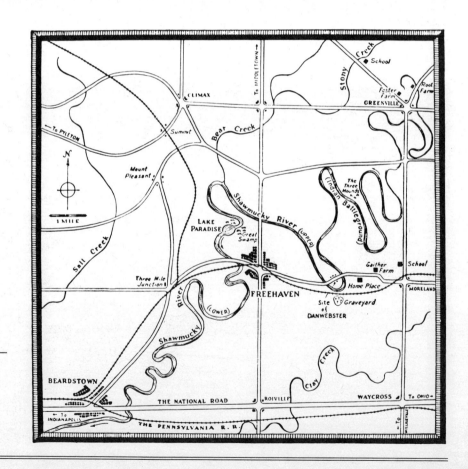

Raintree County (Boston: Houghton Mifflin, 1948) was written by
Ross Lockridge, Jr. (1914–1948). It's one of those panoramic
novels that chronicles a whole people and region. The maps of
Raintree County and Waycross by John Morris serve as excellent
guides to the geography of the story.

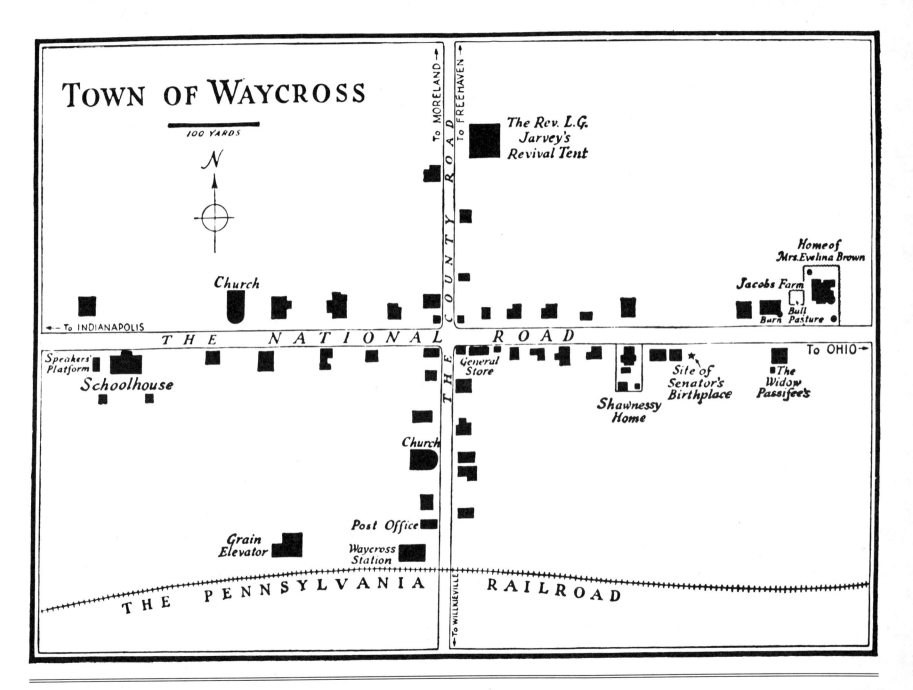

TOWN OF WAYCROSS

100 YARDS

N

Church

← To INDIANAPOLIS

To MORELAND | **To FREEHAVEN**

The Rev. L.G. Jarvey's Revival Tent

Home of Mrs. Evelina Brown

Jacobs Farm

Barn | Bull Pasture

THE NATIONAL ROAD

Speakers' Platform

Schoolhouse

General Store

Site of Senator's Birthplace

The Widow Passifee's

Shawnessy Home

Church

Post Office

Grain Elevator

Waycross Station

To OHIO →

THE COUNTY ROAD

THE PENNSYLVANIA RAILROAD

To WILLKIEVILLE

NARNIA

The world of Narnia was created by C. S. Lewis (1898–1963) from
bits of childhood fantasy and adult allegory in a cycle of seven
novels published from 1950 to 1956 by Macmillan. It is a world
visited on rare occasions by select children, and peopled by talking
beasts, giants, witches, and other characters out of legend and
myth. One of several interesting doorways into Narnia from our
world is through the back of an old closet.

The first map is by J. J. Boies of Staten Island and shows how
a reader has viewed the land. The second map is a reproduction of
Lewis' own map now in the Bodleian Library. The third map of
Narnia has recently been published as a poster by Macmillan.
Drawn by Pauline Baynes, and extremely attractive, the latter
probably will eventually become the definitive rendering.

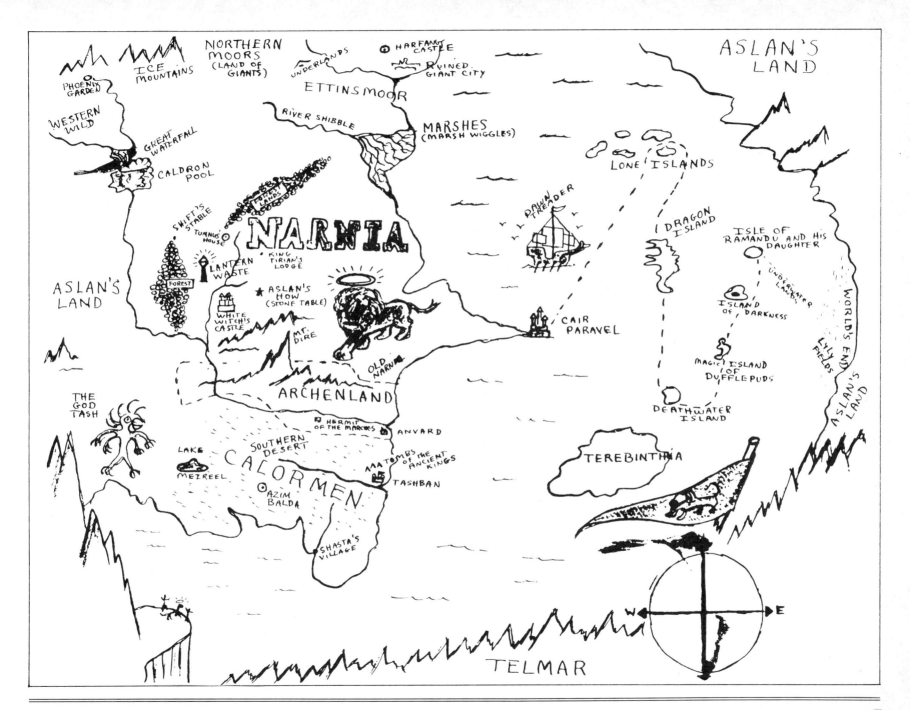

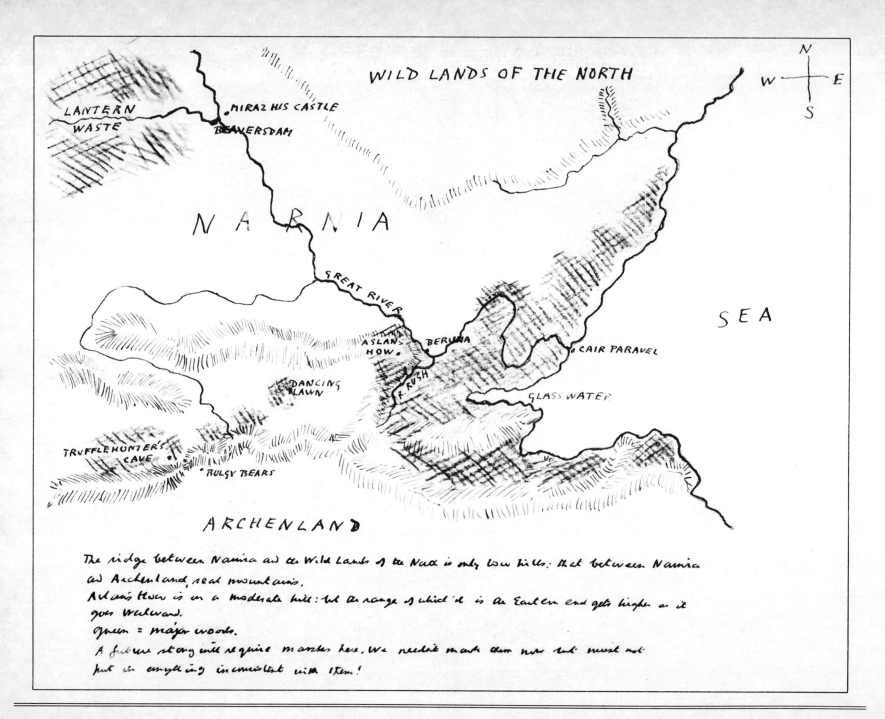

WILD LANDS OF THE NORTH

N
W · E
S

LANTERN
WASTE

· MIRAZ HIS CASTLE

BEAVERSDAM

N A R N I A

GREAT RIVER

SEA

ASLANS
HOW ·

BERUNA

· CAIR PARAVEL

DANCING
LAWN

R. RUSH

GLASS WATER

TRUFFLEHUNTER'S
CAVE ·

· BULGY BEARS

ARCHENLAND

The ridge between Narnia and the Wild Lands of the North is only low hills: that between Narnia
and Archenland, real mountains.

Aslan's How is on a moderate hill: but the range of which it is the Eastern end gets higher as it
goes Westward.

green = major woods.

A future story will require marshes here. We needn't mark them now but must not
put in anything inconsistent with them!

DALARNA

The Well of the Unicorn (New York: William Sloane, 1948) by
"George U. Fletcher" (Fletcher Pratt) is the chronicle of Airar
Alvarson, who has been dispossessed of his farm in Vastmanstad
by the conquering Vulking overlords. He travels around, joining a
resistance movement and eventually driving out the Vulking military
presence only to confront the Dzik attacking the Gentebbi Islands.

Rafael Palacios, still creating excellent maps for major book
publishers, is the artist of the Dalarna map. In addition to this map,
which served as the frontispiece of the book, each chapter has a
map showing in greater detail the area where the action took place.

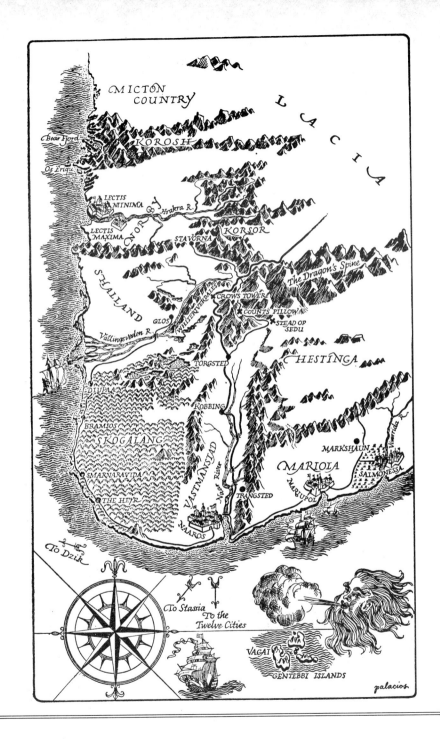

COMMONWEALTH

Silverlock by John Myers Myers, published by E. P. Dutton in 1949, is the story of A. Clarence Shandon who is shipwrecked off the coast of the Commonwealth. In his journey across the island in the company of Golias, who had rescued him from Circe and swinehood in the Archipelago, he meets all manner of men and beasts from legend and classical literature.

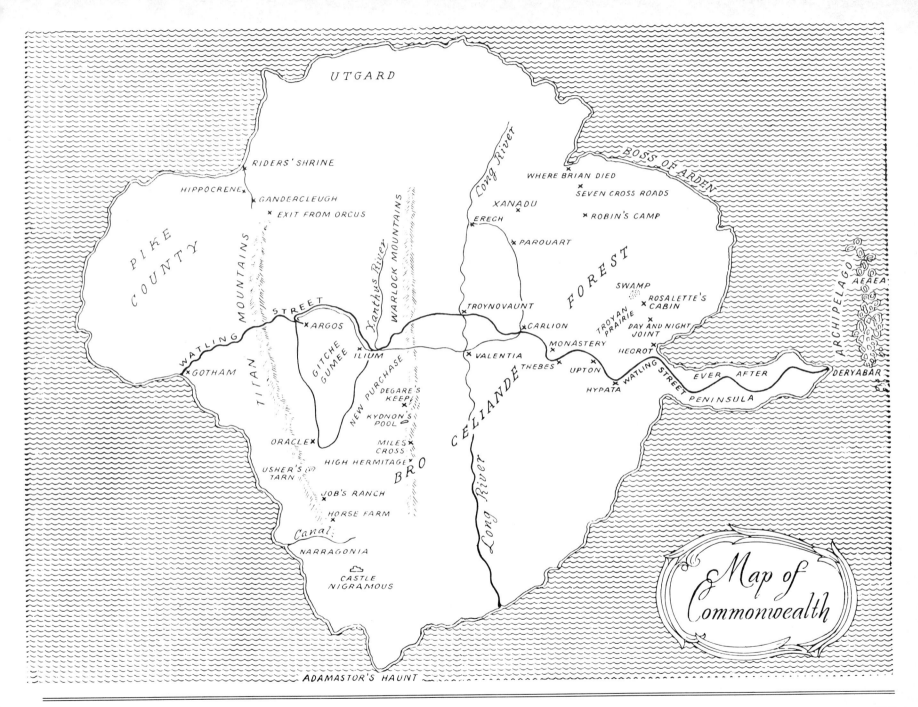

Map of Commonwealth

THE WORLDS OF CAPTAIN FUTURE

Back in the early 1940s Edmond Hamilton created the character Curt Newton, called by everyone "Captain Future." With his faithful companions Simon Wright (a living brain encased in a life-support system), Grag (a robot), and Otho (an android) he strikes fear into the hearts of the evil-doers of the spaceways. Captain Future became such a popular character that an entire magazine was devoted to him, and other writers helped Hamilton chronicle his adventures. A dubious literary immortality was achieved when S. J. Perelman produced "Captain Future, Block That Kick" reprinted in *The Most of S. J. Perelman* (New York: Simon & Schuster, 1958).

Of the maps reproduced here, the Other Side of the Moon is the most interesting. Appearing in the Winter 1942 (Vol. 3, No. 3) issue of *Captain Future,* it was clearly an imaginary map at that time. It is worth comparing this version with an actual map of the other side of the Moon—say, the National Geographic map, *The Earth's Moon* (Washington: National Geographic Society, 1969). The far side of the Moon is rather featureless compared to the near side. The "seas," such a prominent feature of the near side, are lacking on the far side. Anyone describing the far side as it is before the far side was actually mapped would have been accused of having little imagination.

The other maps by no means exhaust the cartography of Captain Future: they are samples. Not shown, for instance, is a diagram of Vulcan, a hollow world circling the sun within the orbit of Mercury. All of the maps reproduced here are from *Captain Future.* For the record, the issues are listed below:

Aar: from Summer 1943 (Vol. 5, No. 3), p. 101.
Eros: from Spring 1942 (Vol. 4, No. 1), p. 95.
Futuria: from Spring 1944 (Vol. 6, No. 2), p. 93.
Mars: from Winter 1941 (Vol. 2, No. 2), p. 95.
Mercury: from Spring 1941 (Vol. 2, No. 3), p. 98.
Moons of Mars: from Fall 1942 (Vol. 4, No. 3), p. 107.
Neptune: from Summer 1940 (Vol. 1, No. 3), p. 122.
Pirates' Planet: from Winter 1942 (Vol. 5, No. 1), p. 107.
Pluto: from Spring 1940 (Vol. 1, No. 2), p. 113.
Saturn: from Fall 1940 (Vol. 2, No. 1), p. 102.
The Twin Planets: from Spring 1943 (Vol. 5, No. 2), p. 103.
Uranus: from Summer 1941 (Vol. 3, No. 1), p. 104.

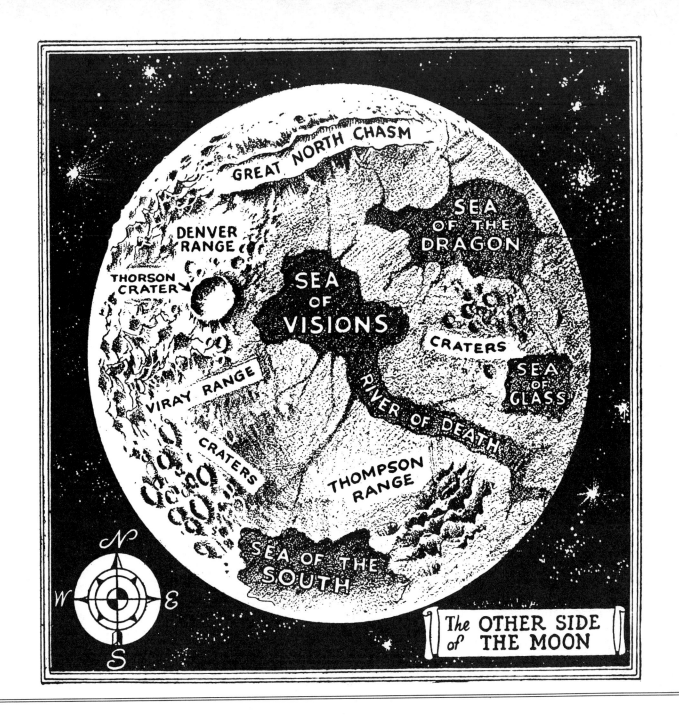

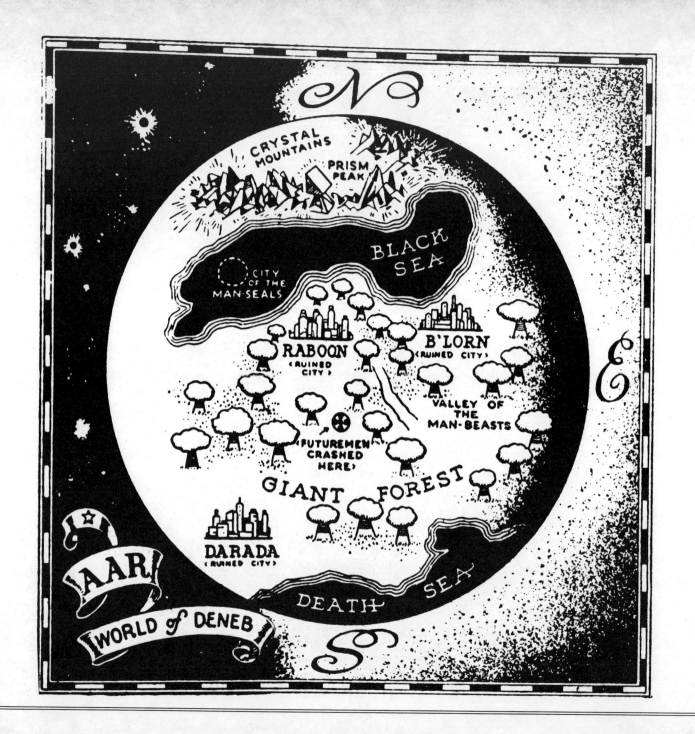

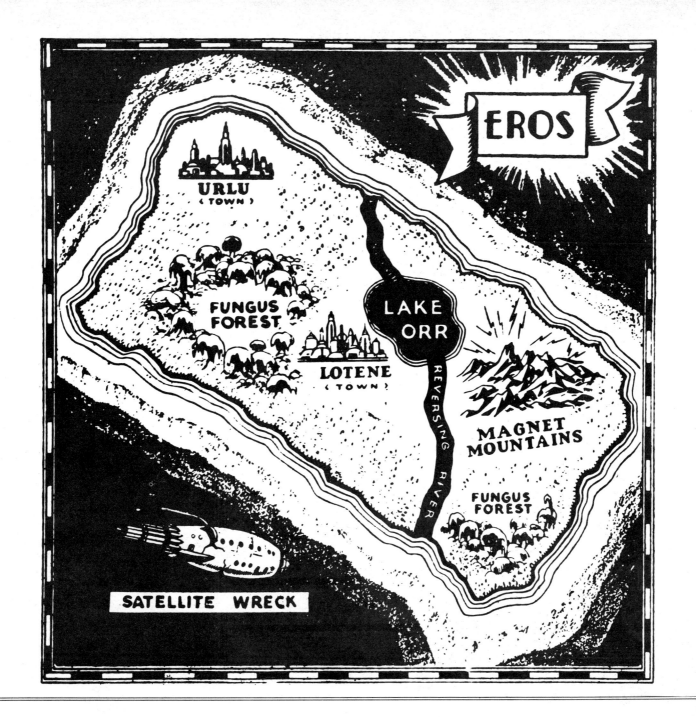

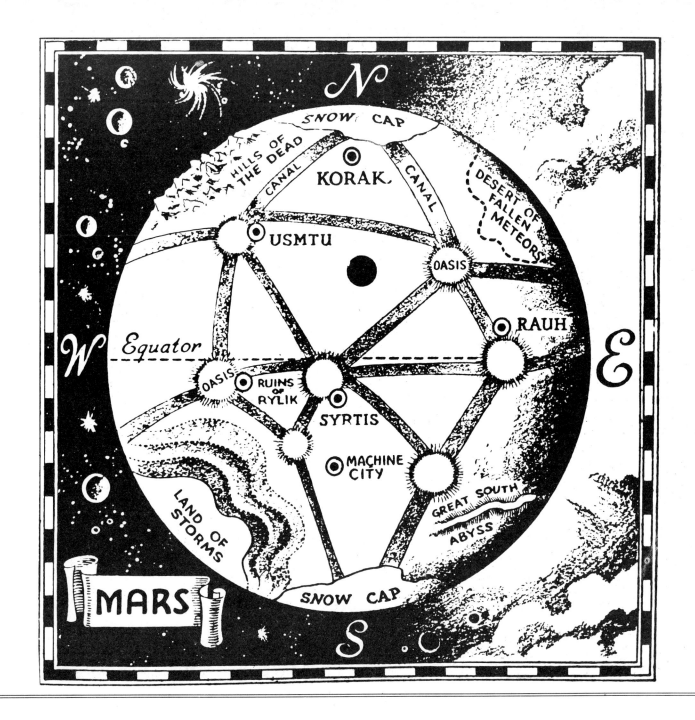

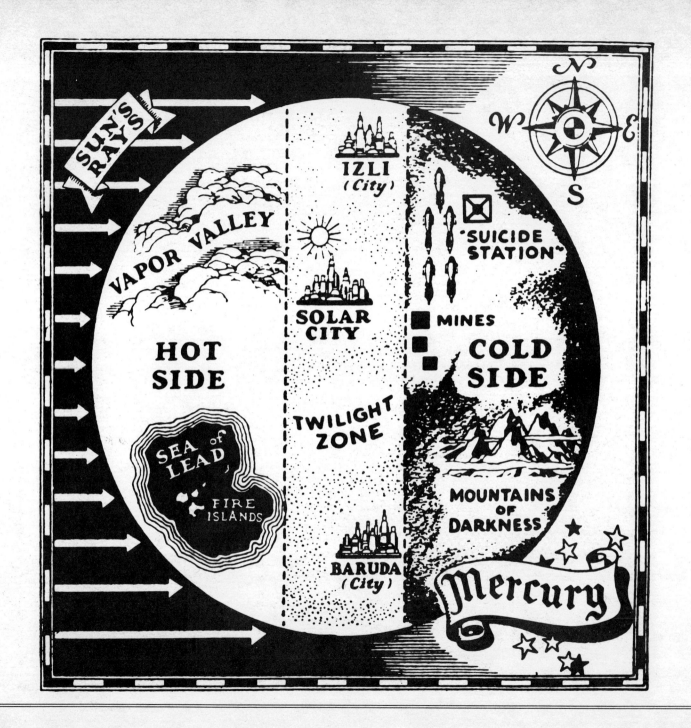

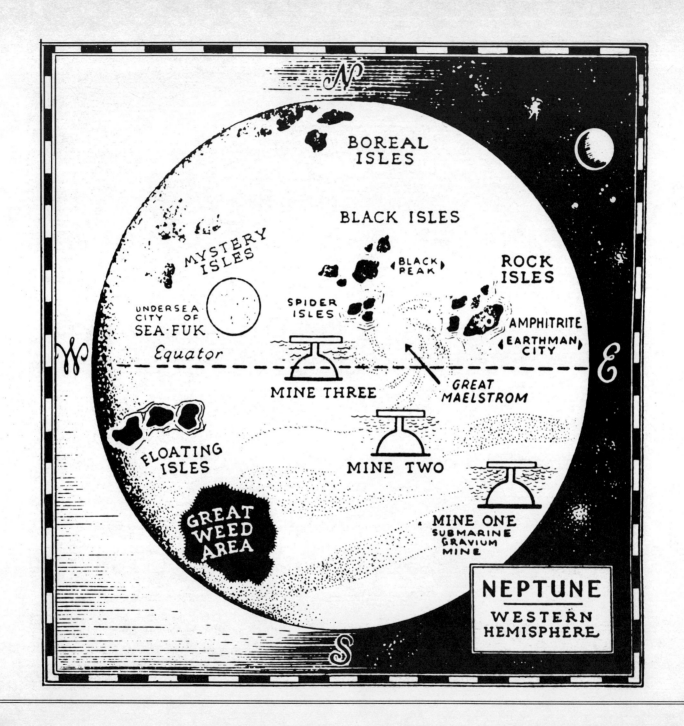

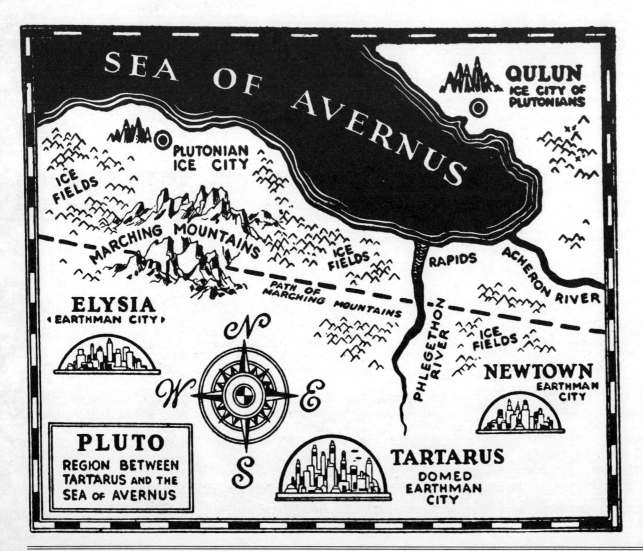

EASTERN
HEMISPHERE
OF PLUTO

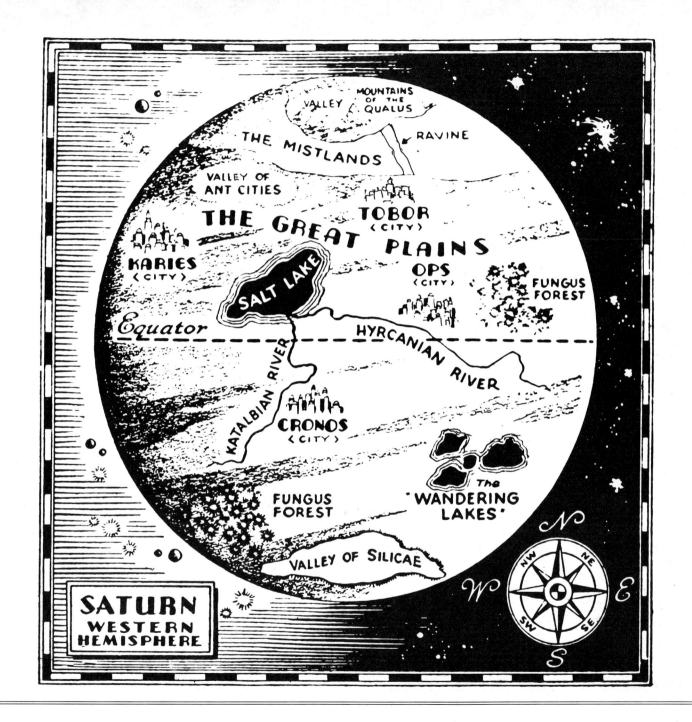

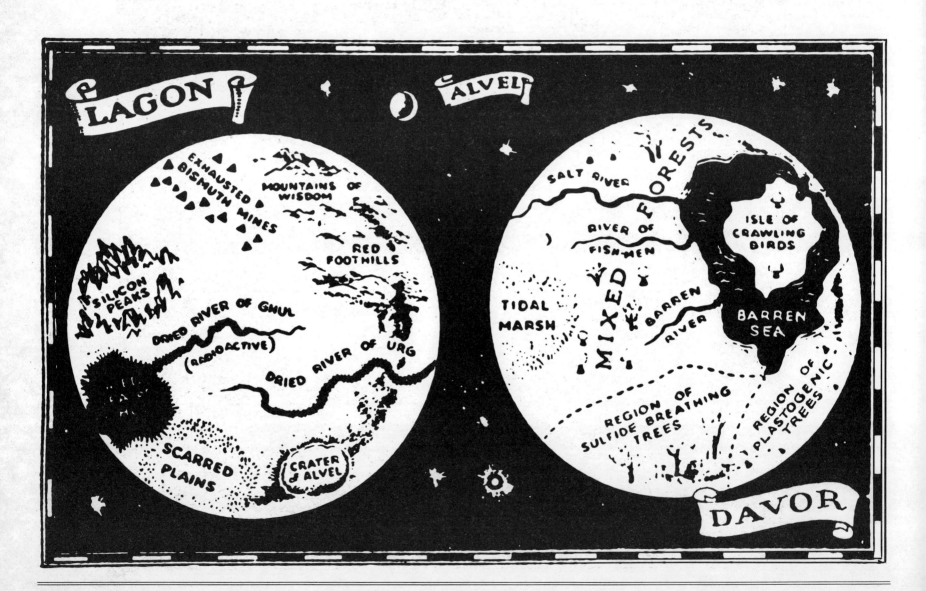

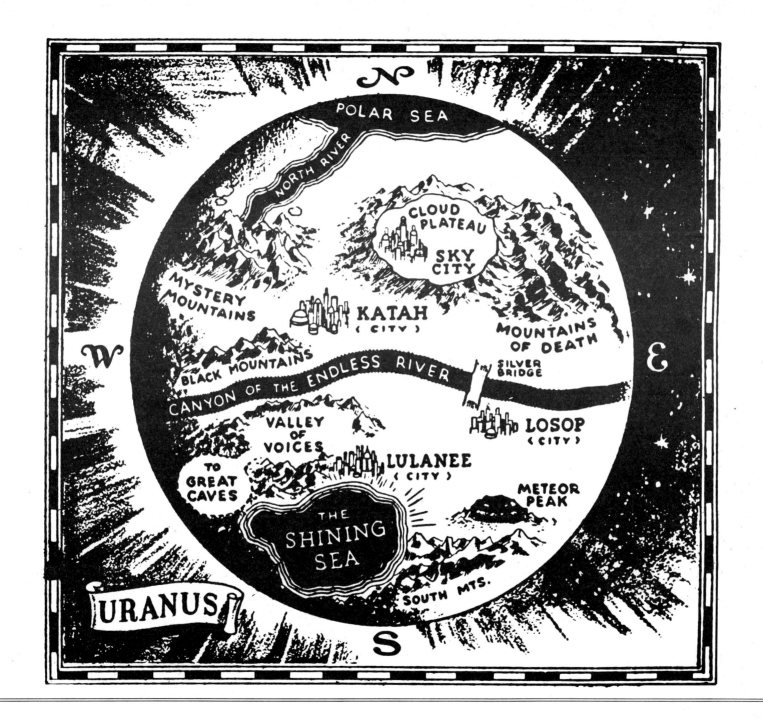

DISPROPORTIONATE MAPS

Again we come to a type of map that is not fantasy in quite the same sense one normally uses the word. The disproportionate map usually has a satiric purpose. In some cases the map is merely an outline of an area with illustrations representing some of the things for which the area is famous—for instance, a map of Wisconsin might have pictures of cheese, cows, and August Derleth. Other examples: a restaurant in Philadelphia, the Pub, has a paper placemat with a map of "Pubadelphia," an amusing parody of Philadelphia. Arnold Roth, the well known cartoonist and artist, has drawn "A Disproportionate Literary View of Philadelphia" jumbling the literary landmarks of Philadelphia together in a clever manner. Copies of the Roth map are for sale in the Rare Book Department of the Free Library of Philadelphia.

The maps reproduced here show the narrow and parochial view of the residents of three areas of the United States.

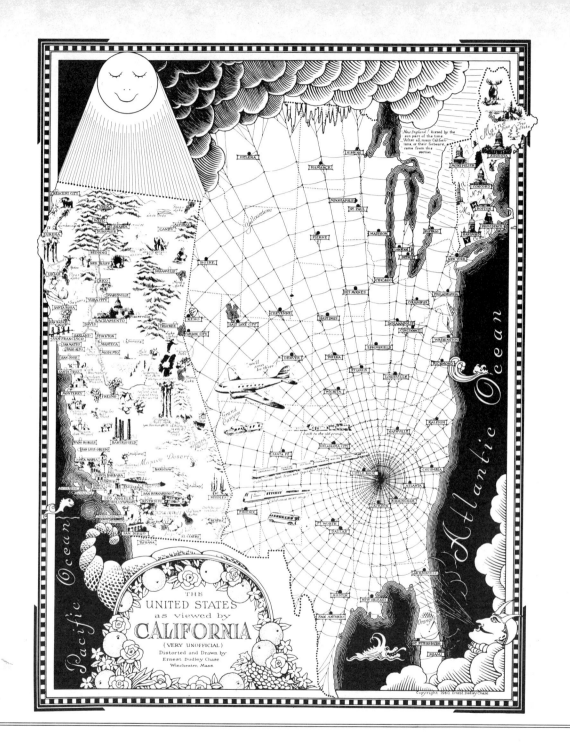

THE
UNITED STATES
as viewed by
CALIFORNIA
(VERY UNOFFICIAL)
Distorted and Drawn by
Ernest Dudley Chase
Winchester, Mass.

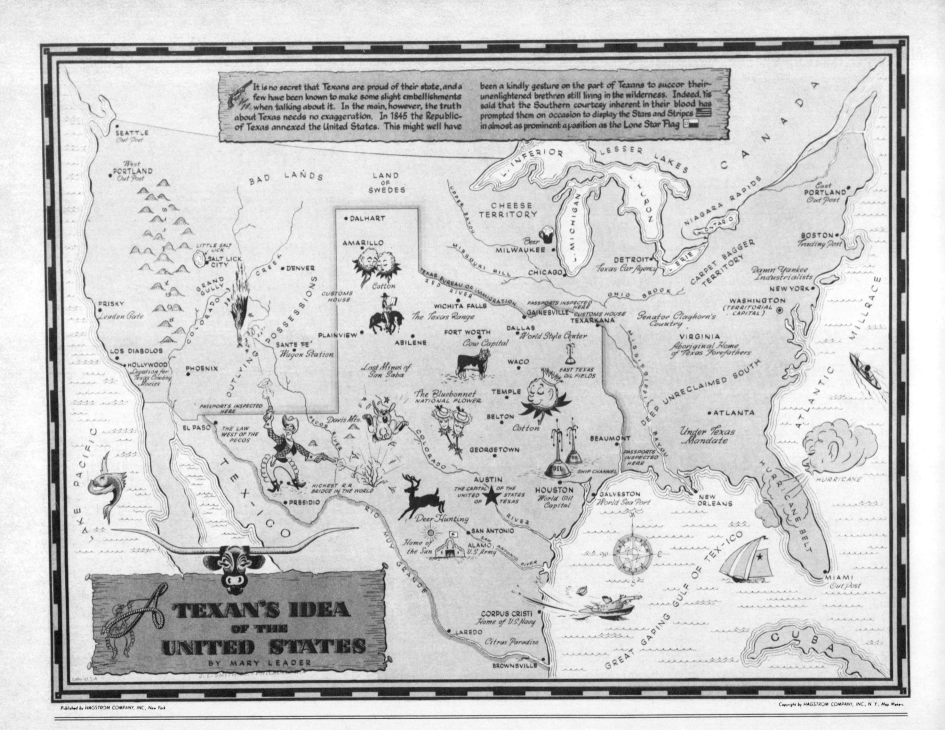

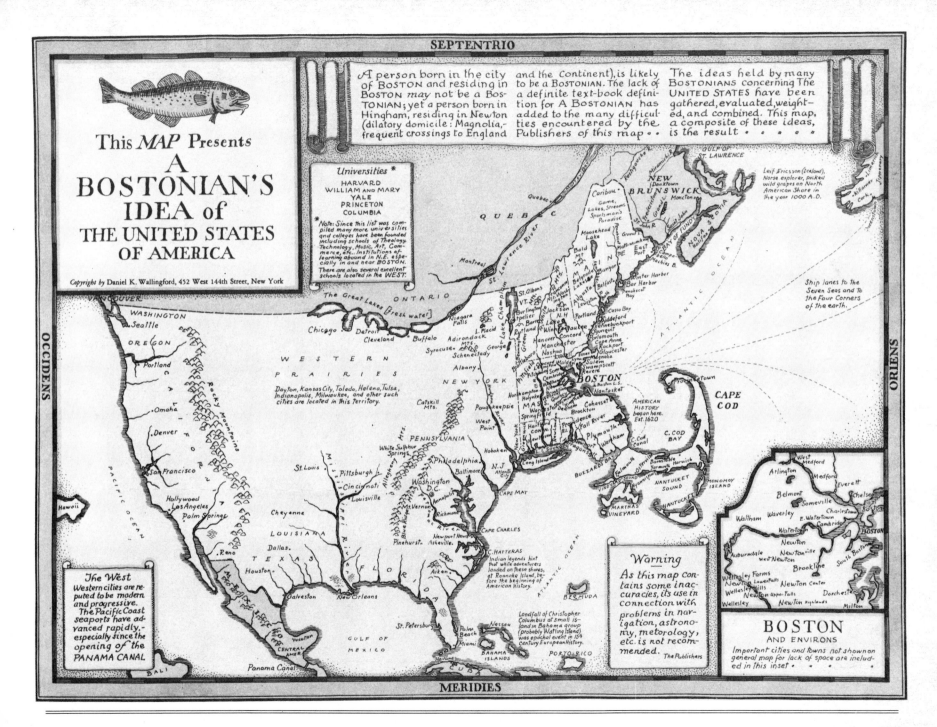

LEIGH BRACKETT'S MARS

Hold on there: we have already had Mars! Well, we have it again
(and again later). Mars, as one of the most popular locations for
science fiction stories, *should* be mapped a lot. This particular Mars
is the Mars of Leigh Brackett. It owes much to the Mars of
Burroughs and is probably first cousin to the Mars of C. L. Moore's
Northwest Smith. It is a dry, inhospitable world, but not yet dead.
Nomads roam the dead sea bottoms and what little civilization
remains clusters around the canal cities. Though writing of several
different characters, Brackett is rather consistent with her planet.
The map is by Margaret M. Howes of Minneapolis, who has several
other fantasy maps not yet published to her credit. Howes has text
accompanying this map in *The Best of Leigh Brackett* (New York:
Ballantine Books, 1977).

Brackett has written stories set on Mercury, Venus, and in
other solar systems. We will deal with Eric John Stark later. For the
moment, let's just note that Mars was one of Brackett's finest
creations. Lin Carter patterned his Mars very much after Brackett's.

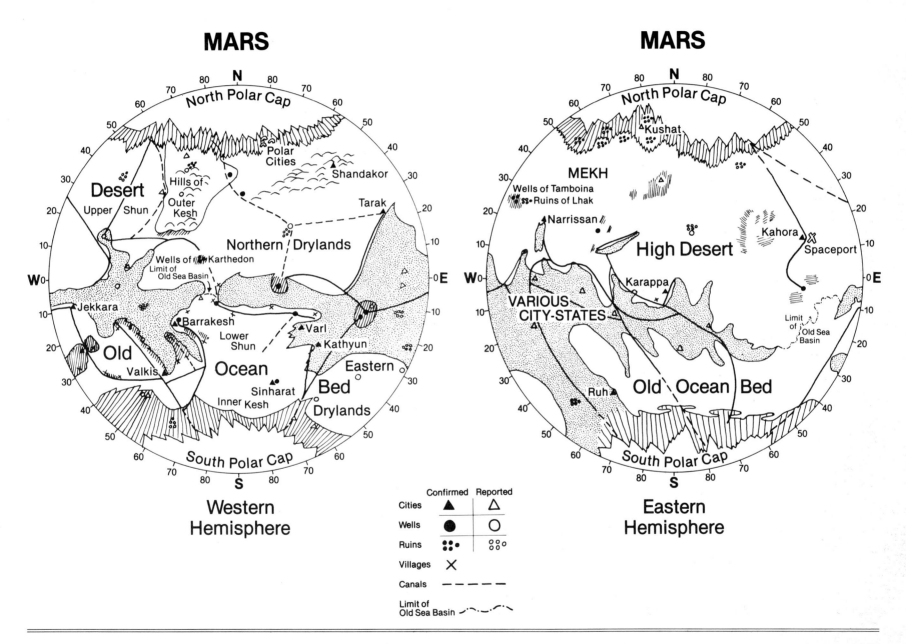

MARS

North Polar Cap

Polar Cities

Shandakor

Desert

Hills of
Outer
Kesh

Upper Shun

Tarak

Northern Drylands

Wells of
Limit of
Old Sea Basin

Karthedon

Jekkara

Barrakesh

Lower
Shun

Varl

Kathyun

Old

Valkis

Ocean

Inner Kesh

Sinharat

Bed

Eastern

Drylands

South Polar Cap

Western Hemisphere

MARS

North Polar Cap

Kushat

MEKH

Wells of Tamboina
Ruins of Lhak

Narrissan

High Desert

Kahora

Spaceport

Karappa

VARIOUS
CITY-STATES

Limit
of
Old Sea
Basin

Ruh

Old Ocean Bed

South Polar Cap

Eastern Hemisphere

	Confirmed	Reported
Cities	▲	△
Wells	●	○
Ruins	∷•	○○○
Villages	✗	
Canals	– – –	
Limit of Old Sea Basin	⌐·⌐·⌐	

LAND BETWEEN THE MOUNTAINS

The inhabitants of the land between the mountains, from Carol Kendall's book, *The Gammage Cup* (New York: Harcourt Brace Jovanovich, 1959), are as complacent and smugly self-satisfied as are the Hobbits of the Shire. They have forgotten their warlike past and flight from the Mushroom People (large-headed mutants?) in the security of their lost valley. The government of Slipper-on-the-Water exiles its most imaginative and energetic citizens into the wilderness, where they discover the Mushroom People entering the valley through abandoned gold mines. The alarm is sounded and the invaders driven off.

The map illustration reproduced here is by Erik Blegvad. As well as many interesting illustrations, the book has a more detailed view of Slipper-on-the-Water.

SLOBBOVIA

Slobbovia, or more particularly, Lower Slobbovia, is the creation of cartoonist Al Capp. For a mountain boy, Li'l Abner is remarkably cosmopolitan in his wanderings. Dogpatch is so depressed that I suspect Slobbovia was devised to make things look good in Dogpatch. The map we have here is the official map of Slobbovia, though that venerable and frigid land has evolved in the years since this map was drawn. There is at least one other map I recall: it was a cross section of Slobbovia showing Slobbovia connected to the ocean floor by a column of ice.

One may wonder why we have a map of Slobbovia but not one of Dogpatch. Quite simply, Dogpatch has not been completely mapped yet. There have been portions of Dogpatch shown, usually in those strips dealing with the annual invasion of the Turnip Termites, or Teetering Rock, or the Sadie Hawkins Day Race. These tend to be aerial views and are not consistent with each other. Dogpatch has, by the way, been located in or near the Ozark Mountains. Episodes dealing with outside influences on Dogpatch have shown a map of the United States with Dogpatch pinpointed in the Ozark region. Sorry, but I can not offer any suggestions about the geographical relationship between Dogpatch and Snuffy Smith's turf.

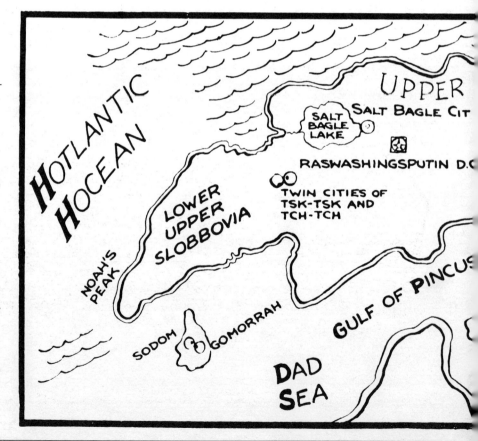

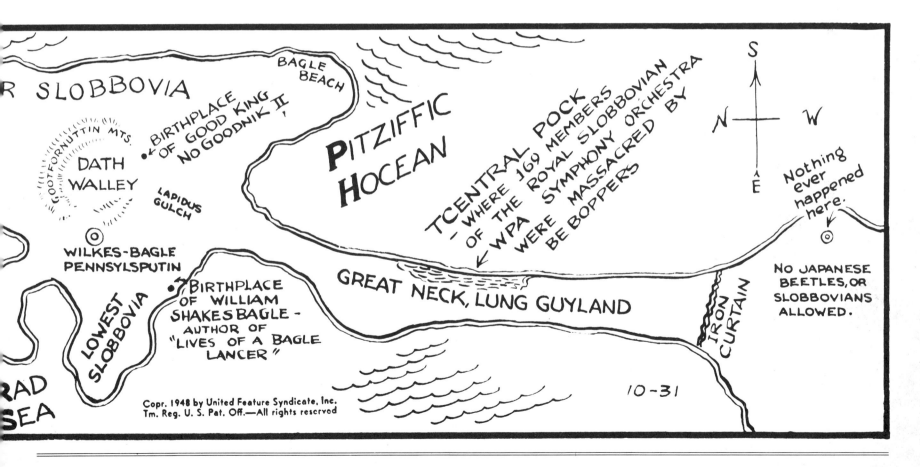

HYPERBOREA

The magazine *Weird Tales* contained stories by obscure writers as well as some who became well known, but looking back through the mists of time three writers seem to have dominated it: H. P. Lovecraft, Robert E. Howard, and Clark Ashton Smith. Smith (1893–1961) ranks with Lord Dunsany and James Branch Cabell in his mastery of word weaving. Indeed, he considered himself a poet first and foremost. The Book Club of California published a collection of his verse early in its existence. In prose fiction he was quite versatile and inventive. Perhaps his creation of worlds can not match Edgar Rice Burroughs, but several worlds rolled from his pen. Hyperborea is an early prehistoric continent, the first land to be inhabited by humans. The stories of Hyperborea cover much of its history and have been assembled in chronological order by Lin Carter in *Hyperborea* (New York: Ballantine Books, 1971) from which this map is taken with Mr. Carter's permission and blessings.

The stories of Clark Ashton Smith are characterized by a pleasantly morbid outlook, by what we would now call "black humor." Heroes are beaten and defeated as often as in the works of Lord Dunsany, but they are all the more amusing because they are cast in a fairytale format.

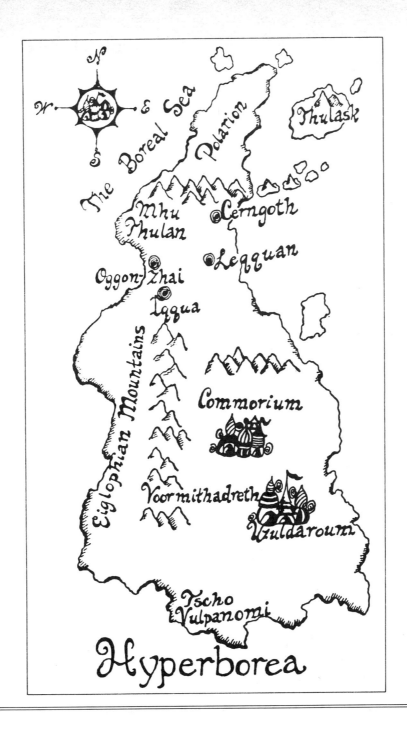

Hyperborea

ZOTHIQUE

From Hyperborea, the first land, we come to Zothique, the last continent on a dying Earth. Here, once more, magic and wizardry reign as Mankind waits for the end. This map was drawn by L. Sprague de Camp. It notes the relationship of Zothique to the present Eurasian land mass. Between Hyperborea and Zothique in time Clark Ashton Smith wrote a series of stories set in a sinking Atlantis, and another in the medieval land of Averoigne. He began a series set on Mars and started to create another solar system, but these worlds were left fragmentary and not fully realized.

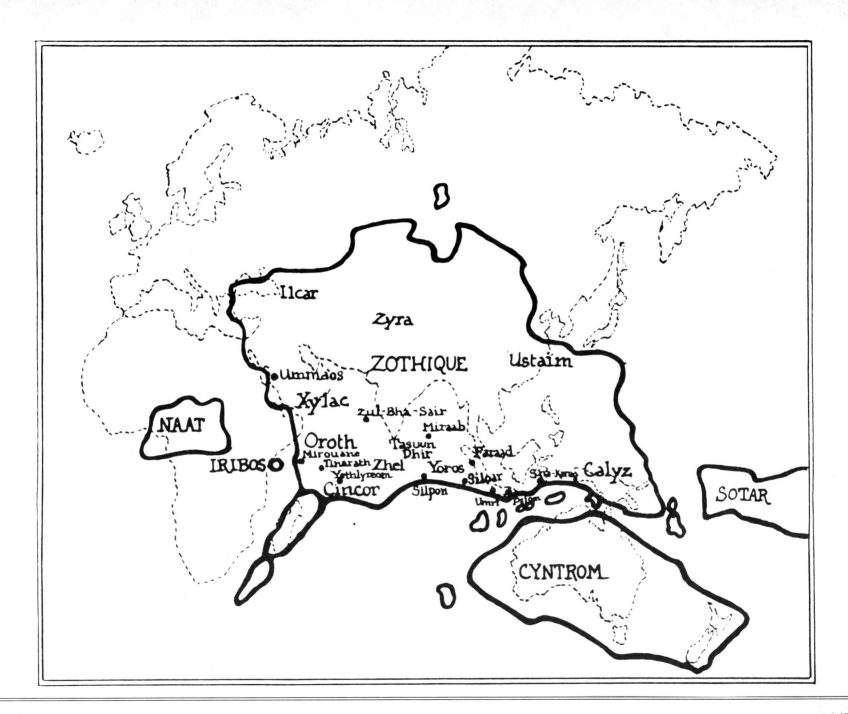

Ilcar

Zyra

ZOTHIQUE

Ustaim

•Ummaos

Xylac

Zul-Bha-Sair

Miraab

NAAT

Oroth

Tasuun

Dhir

Faraad

Mirouane

Tinarath Zhel

Yoros

Sixô-Kang

Calyz

IRIBOSO

Yethlyreom

Silpar

SOTAR

Cincor

Silpon

Umri Pilgom

CYNTROM

QUIVERA

Other writers have written of lost treasures and pirate intrigue.
Vaughan Wilkins' *The City of Frozen Fire* (New York: Macmillan,
1951) combines a pirate yarn with a lost race tale. Lost race stories
revolve around some group—Ancient Greeks, Romans, Vikings,
subhumans, Atlanteans, ancient Egyptians, or unknown
peoples—surviving into modern times in some obscure and
forgotten corner of the world. Wilkins picks the Welsh under Madoc
setting sail in the 12th Century and vanishing from history.
Somewhere in South America is the land of Quivera where the
Welsh have settled. Swamps, jungles, and mountains hem them in
on the landward side while sheer cliffs protect them on the seaward
side. In the 1820s these Welsh rescue a wrecked ship's crew and
learn, to their sorrow, of gunpowder. The villains ravage the land
and loot the ruby mines but find themselves cut off from escape.
The current prince, also called Madoc, sets sail to find help for the
Quiverians. After some misadventures he finds the family of
Christopher Standish and enlists them in his cause. The story is fast
moving and entertaining.

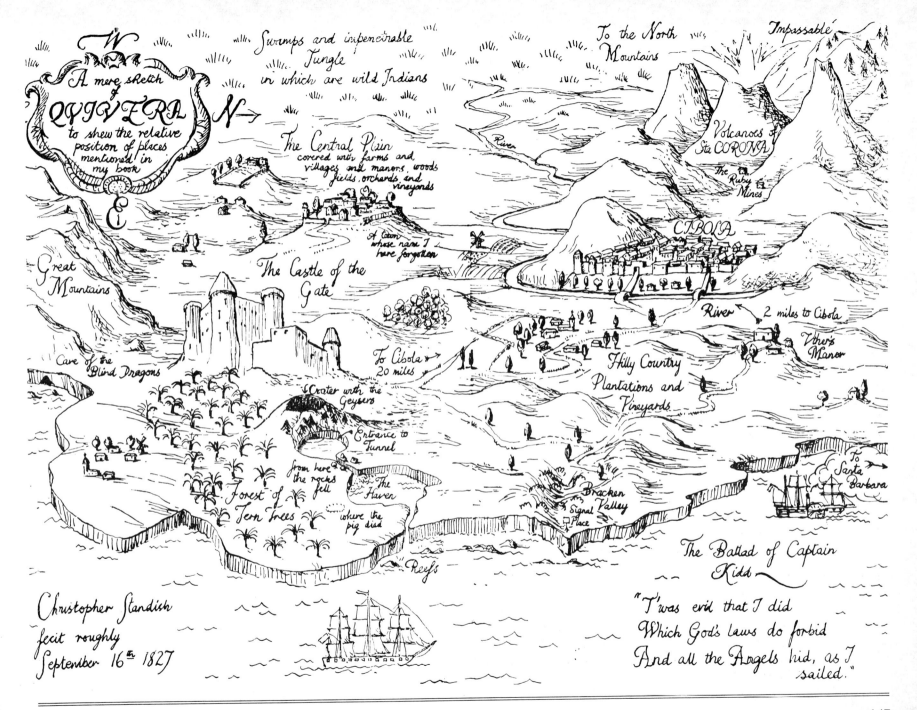

W

A mere sketch of QVIVERA to shew the relative position of places mentioned in my book

N→

E

Swamps and impenetrable Jungle in which are wild Indians

To the North Mountains

Impassable

River

Volcanoes of Sta CORONA

The Ruby Mines

The Central Plain covered with farms and villages and manors, woods, fields, orchards and vineyards

A town whose name I have forgotten

CIBOLA

Great Mountains

The Castle of the Gate

River

2 miles to Cibola

Cave of the Blind Dragons

To Cibola 20 miles

Hilly Country Plantations and Vineyards

Vther's Manor

Crater with the Geysers

Entrance to Tunnel

from here the rocks fell

The Haven

Forest of Tern Trees

where the pig died

Bracken Valley

Signal Place

To Santa Barbara

Reefs

The Ballad of Captain Kidd

Christopher Standish fecit roughly September 16th 1827

"T'was evil that I did Which God's laws do forbid And all the Angels hid, as I sailed."

JEFFERSON, YOKNAPATAWPHA COUNTY, MISSISSIPPI

William Faulkner (1897–1962) wrote of the lives of the inhabitants of Yoknapatawpha County, Mississippi. The county seat, Jefferson, was partially modeled after Oxford, Mississippi, but Faulkner moulded Jefferson into its own world. Herewith mapped, the environs of Jefferson stand out in all their starkness. This map, which appeared as the endpaper of *Absalom, Absalom!* (New York: Random House, 1936), is well annotated and self-explanatory for anyone who has read the stories. If the map is confusing; well, go thou and read.

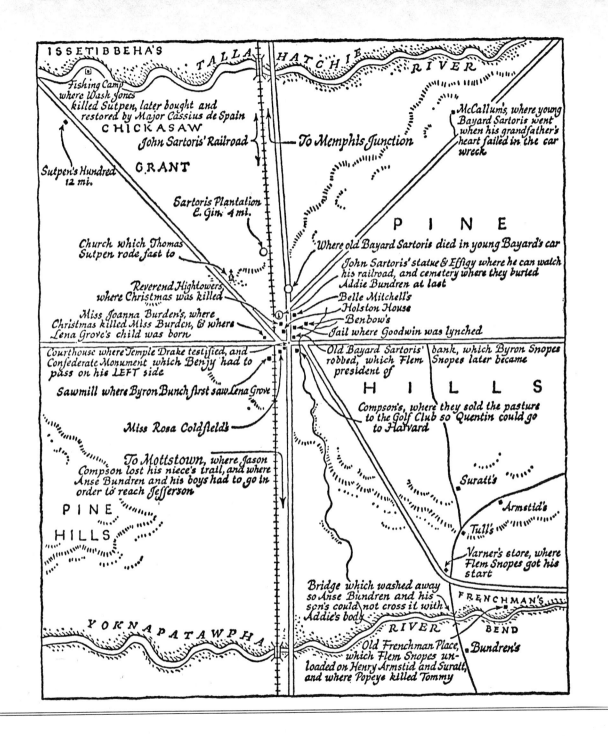

ISSETIBBEHA'S   TALLA HATCHIE   RIVER

Fishing Camp
where Wash Jones
killed Sutpen, later bought and
restored by Major Cassius de Spain

CHICKASAW

John Sartoris' Railroad

GRANT

Sutpen's Hundred
12 mi.

Sartoris Plantation
& Gin. 4 mi.

Church which Thomas
Sutpen rode fast to

Reverend Hightower's,
where Christmas was killed

Miss Joanna Burden's, where
Christmas killed Miss Burden, & where
Lena Grove's child was born

Courthouse where Temple Drake testified, and
Confederate Monument which Benjy had to
pass on his LEFT side

Sawmill where Byron Bunch first saw Lena Grove

Miss Rosa Coldfield's

To Mottstown, where Jason
Compson lost his niece's trail, and where
Anse Bundren and his boys had to go in
order to reach Jefferson

PINE

HILLS

YOKNAPATAWPHA

To Memphis Junction

McCallum's, where young
Bayard Sartoris went
when his grandfather's
heart failed in the car
wreck.

PINE

Where old Bayard Sartoris died in young Bayard's car

John Sartoris' statue & Effigy where he can watch
his railroad, and cemetery where they buried
Addie Bundren at last
Belle Mitchell's
Holston House
Benbow's
Jail where Goodwin was lynched

Old Bayard Sartoris' bank, which Byron Snopes
robbed, which Flem Snopes later became
president of

HILLS

Compson's, where they sold the pasture
to the Golf Club so Quentin could go
to Harvard

Suratt's

Armstid's

Tull's

Varner's store, where
Flem Snopes got his
start

Bridge which washed away
so Anse Bundren and his
son's could not cross it with
Addie's body

FRENCHMAN'S

RIVER   BEND

Bundren's

Old Frenchman Place,
which Flem Snopes un-
loaded on Henry Armstid and Suratt,
and where Popeye killed Tommy

THE WITCH WORLD

The Witch World is a place far removed from Earth in time and space. The Earthman, Simon Tregarth, arrives through the Gates between Alizon and Estcarp. Because he has some psychic powers lacking in men of this world, he immediately comes into conflict with the witch women who dominate Estcarp. They reluctantly use him in a fight with the Kolder, an alien people of advanced technology fleeing disaster in their own world through their own set of Gates, and who are attempting to dominate the Witch World.

The map is by Barbara Johnson based on the series of novels by André Norton. Ace Books, the current publisher of Miss Norton's stories, has issued a copy of the map to accompany a boxed set of Witch World novels.

Map of the Witch World

Alizon

Estcarp

Escore

Karsten

Gorm

HI-IAY
ISLANDS

Parodies of scientific works abound. The dead seriousness and somberness of most scientific reports invites the satirist to enliven matters with fun-poking, both in style and subject matter. Gerolf Steiner, under the name "Harald Stumke," has written and illustrated the entertaining spoof *The Snouters* (Garden City, N.Y.: Natural History Press, 1967). The Snouters are a class of beings (with the technical name of *Rhinogrades,* so called because they have elongated proboscises) existing only in the Hi-Iay Islands. The book is done in a serious manner, complete with bibliography, and describes the varieties of Rhinogrades and their habits. The map is ideal for the parody.

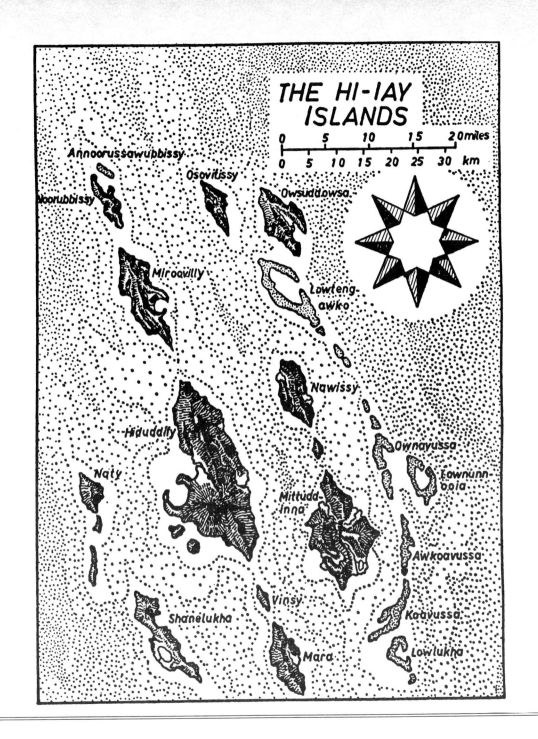

THE HI-IAY
ISLANDS

0   5   10   15   20 miles
0   5   10   15   20   25   30 km

Annoorussawubbissy

Osovitissy

Owsuddowso

Noorubbissy

Miroavilly

Lowteng-
awko

Nawissy

Hiduddify

Ownayussa

Naty

Lownunn-
ooia

Mittudd-
Inna

Awkoavussa

Vinsy

Shanelukha

Koavussa

Mara

Lowlukha

EARTHSEA

Ursula K. Le Guin is a remarkable author noted for the creation of a whole galactic civilization in some of her stories. In *A Wizard of Earthsea* (New York: Bantam, 1975) she creates a world of islands where magic works. Ged, a young apprentice wizard, releases a terrible force and spends the rest of the book hunting it down and nullifying it. Mrs. Le Guin creates a coherent world with its own folklore and legends. Like *The Lord of the Rings* and *The Once and Future King,* this is no mere children's book, but a major work of fantasy—a classic. A sequel takes Ged to the Tombs of Atuan. A third tale, *The Farthest Shore* (New York: Bantam, 1975), has an older Ged save the world from a dread power.

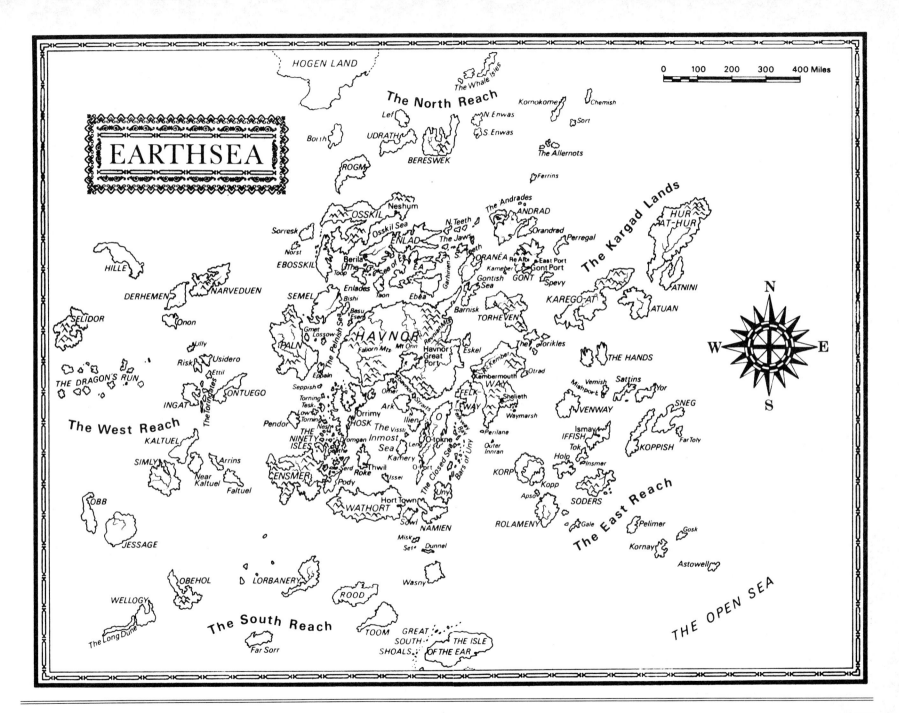

EARTHSEA

HOGEN LAND

The Whale Isles

The North Reach

Kornokomer   Chemish

Lef   N Enwas   Sort

Borth   S Enwas

UDRATH

ROGM   BERESWEK   The Allernots

Ferrins

Neshum

OSSKIL   The Andrades

Sorresk   ANDRAD

Osskil Sea   N. Teeth   Orandrad   The Kargad Lands

Norst   ENLAD   The Jaw   Perregal   HUR AT-HUR

Berila   S. Teeth   Teeth   ORANÉA   Re Albi   East Port

HILLE   EBOSSKIL   Toop   Sea of Éa   ÉA   Kameber   Gont Port

DERHEMEN   NARVEDUEN   Onon   SEMEL   Enlades   Gontish   GONT   Spevy   ATNINI

Bishi   Taon   Ebéa   Sea   Garhiren

SELIDOR   Besu   Barnisk   KAREGO-AT   ATUAN

Gmet   Esem   HAVNOR   TORHEVEN

Lossow   Remma Mts.

PALN   Faliern Mts.   Mt Onn   The Torikles

Ully   Havnor   Eskel   THE HANDS

Risk   Usidero   Great   R. Kember

THE DRAGON'S RUN   Ettil   Port   Kembermouth   Otrad   Mishport   Vemish   Sattins   N

INGAT   ONTUEGO   Eppain   WAY   Shelieth   VENWAY   Yor   W   E

The West Reach   Torning   Seppish   Other   FELK   Waymarsh   SNEG   S

Tesk   Ark   Straits   WAY   FarToly

KALTUEL   Low   Torning   Orrimy   Ilien   Perilane   Ismay   KOPPISH

Pendor   HOSK   The   Vissti   IFFISH

SIMLY   Near   THE   Nesh   Inmost   O-tokne   Outer   Tok

Kaltuel   Arrins   NINETY   Dromgan   Leng   Sea   Innran   Holp   Insmer

ISLES   Gath   KORP

Serd   Thwil   O Port   KORNAY

CENSMER   Roke   Issel   Uny   Kopp   SODERS

OBB   Pody   Apso

Hort Town   ROLAMENY   Gale   Pelimer   Gosk

JESSAGE   WATHORT   The East Reach

Sowl   NAMIEN   Kornay

WELLOGY   Misk   Astowell

Set   Dunnel

The Long Dune   OBEHOL   LORBANERY   Wasny

The South Reach   ROOD   THE OPEN SEA

Far Sorr   TOOM   GREAT

SOUTH   THE ISLE

SHOALS   OF THE EAR

0   100   200   300   400 Miles

THE
LANDS
BEYOND

In Norton Juster's *The Phantom Tollbooth* (New York: Random House, 1961) with illustrations by Jules Feiffer, we have another allegorical children's book. Milo is a little boy bored with everything. One day he receives a mysterious gift: a Phantom Tollbooth. Assembling it (yes, it came unassembled) he drives through it in his car to the Lands Beyond. Becoming lost in the Doldrums, land of the Lethargarians, he is saved by Tock, a dog with a clock for a body—a watch dog. Together they journey to Dictionopolis and run afoul of the fascist Short Shrift who flings them in a dungeon. The whole book is a series of puns and plays on words, some of them pretty awful. In the end Milo is no longer bored and returns to the real world vowing to pay more attention to words and numbers.

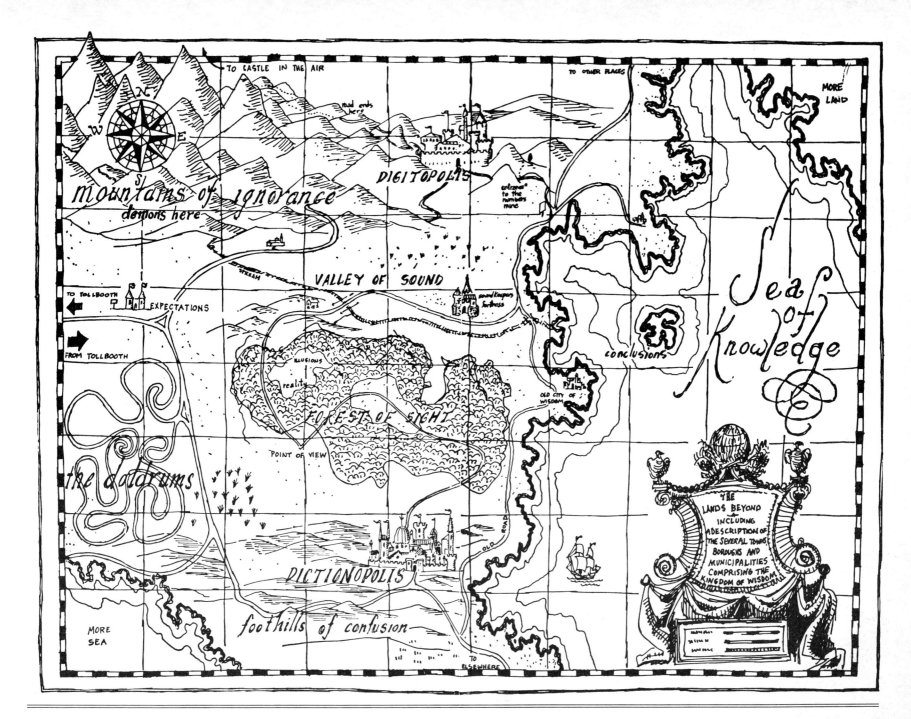

SECRET WORLD OF OG

Pierre Berton's *The Secret World of Og* (Boston: Little, Brown, 1962), illustrated by William Winter, is one of those children's books adults can enjoy. Penny, Pam, Patty, Peter, Paul, Yukon King (a dog), and Earless Osdick (a cat) have an adventure in a world under their playhouse, a world of little green men and lost toys. The story line is simple: Paul and Earless Osdick are kidnapped by the Green Men, and the other children (and Yukon King) save them. The characters are based on Berton's own family, and each has a distinctive personality. Adults will enjoy the loving descriptions of mannerisms.

DILFAR AND ENVIRONS

Roger Zelazny (1937–   ) composed a cycle of tales about
Dilvish the Damned who returned from Hell to protect his country
from danger. While abounding with atmosphere and quite readable,
the stories will appeal more to the *cognoscente* than to the general
reader. It is interesting to note on the map that the artist has
lettered "Portardy" when it should be "Portaroy." The map is
reproduced from *Warlocks and Warriors* (New York: Putnam, 1970).

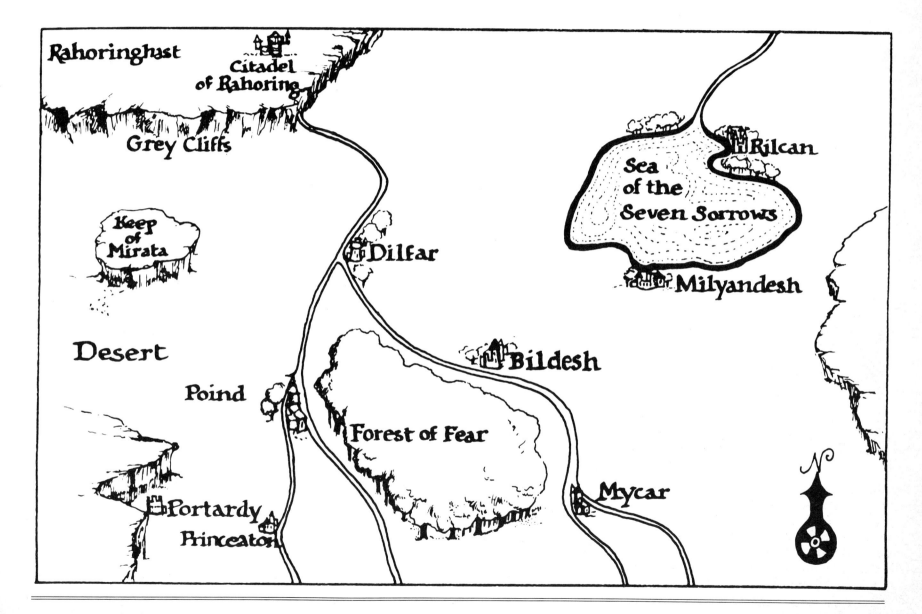

THE YOUNG
KINGDOMS

Elric of Melnibone and his enchanted (cursed, rather) sword, Stormbringer, wander about the Young Kingdoms in an ancient prehistoric time. Elric is a weak albino who takes on the strength of the men killed by Stormbringer. Michael Moorcock, who wrote the stories, is a versatile British author of a wide variety of writing ranging from blood-and-thunder adventure tales to obscurely written modern novels. The saga of Elric is an example of how a series evolves and ends at a different point than the author intended. Starting out as a mere adventure series, it ends with a Gotterdammerung of the forces of Chaos. This map is by John Collier and Walter Romanski.

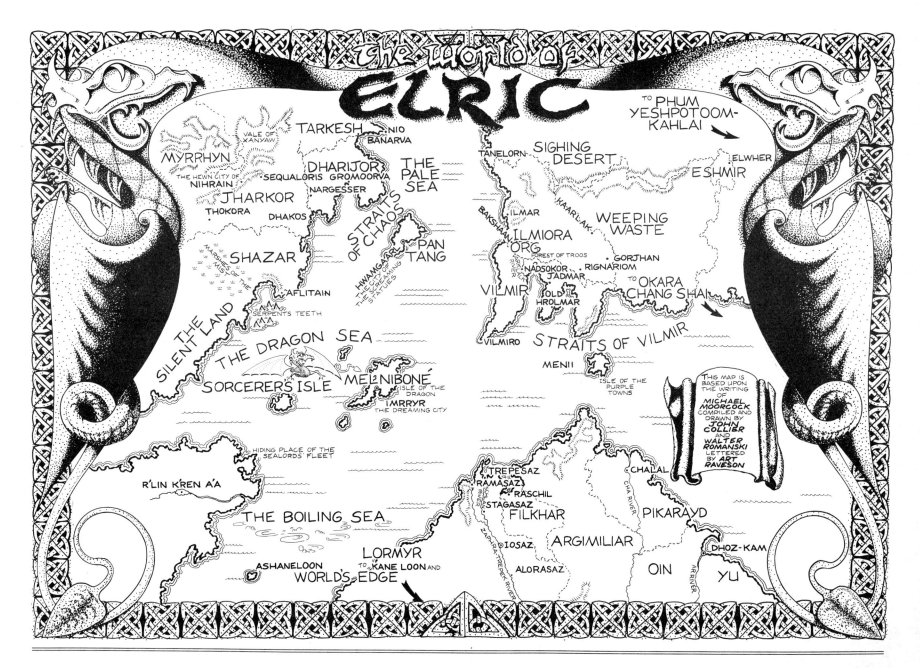

The World of **ELRIC**

TO PHUM
YESHPOTOOM-
KAHLAI

VALE OF XANYAW
TARKESH
NIO
BANARVA

MYRRHYN

THE HEWN CITY OF NIHRAIN

DHARIJOR
SEQUALORIS GROMOORVA
NARGESSER

THE PALE SEA

JHARKOR
THOKORA
DHAKOS

STRAITS OF CHAOS

SHAZAR

MARSHES OF THE MIST

AFLITAIN

PAN TANG

HWAMGAA, THE CITY OF THE SCREAMING STATUES

SERPENTS TEETH

THE SILENT LAND

THE DRAGON SEA

SORCERER'S ISLE

MEL'NIBONÉ
ISLE OF THE DRAGON

IMRRYR
THE DREAMING CITY

R'LIN K'REN A'A

HIDING PLACE OF THE SEALORDS' FLEET

THE BOILING SEA

ASHANELOON

LORMYR
TO KANE LOON AND
WORLD'S EDGE

TANELORN

SIGHING DESERT

ELWHER
ESHMIR

ILMAR

KAARLAK

WEEPING WASTE

BAKSHAAN

ILMIORA
ORG
FOREST OF TROOS

GORJHAN

NADSOKOR
JADMAR

RIGNARIOM

VILMIR

OLD HROLMAR

TO OKARA
CHANG SHAI

VILMIRO

STRAITS OF VILMIR

MENII

ISLE OF THE PURPLE TOWNS

CHALAL

TREPESAZ
RAMASAZ
RASCHIL
STAGASAZ

FILKHAR

CHA RIVER

PIKARAYD

ZAPHRA-TREPEK RIVER

IOSAZ

ARGIMILIAR

DHOZ-KAM

ALORASAZ

OIN

AR RIVER

YU

THIS MAP IS BASED UPON THE WRITING OF MICHAEL MOORCOCK COMPILED AND DRAWN BY JOHN COLLIER AND WALTER ROMANSKI LETTERED BY ART RAVESON

163

THE DYING EARTH

Quite similar in mood and theme to Zothique is the saga of dying
Earth chronicled by Jack Vance in his *The Dying Earth,* first
published in 1950. The book is a series of stories laid on an Earth
at the end of its life when the remnant of humanity loses itself in
debauchery to stave off thoughts of the coming end. Magic, often
the last remnant of an advanced technology, is the interest of a few
people. The scenery is described in a language that can only be
called "lush."

This map by George Barr is the endpaper decoration for the
elegant, illustrated edition of *The Dying Earth* (San Francisco and
Columbia, Penn.: Underwood-Miller, 1976). Another version of the
area of Grand Motholam appeared in *Amra,* and that map, by
Robert Briney, was used in the first edition of *An Atlas of
Fantasy.* While the two maps agree in many particulars, they
disagree in others.

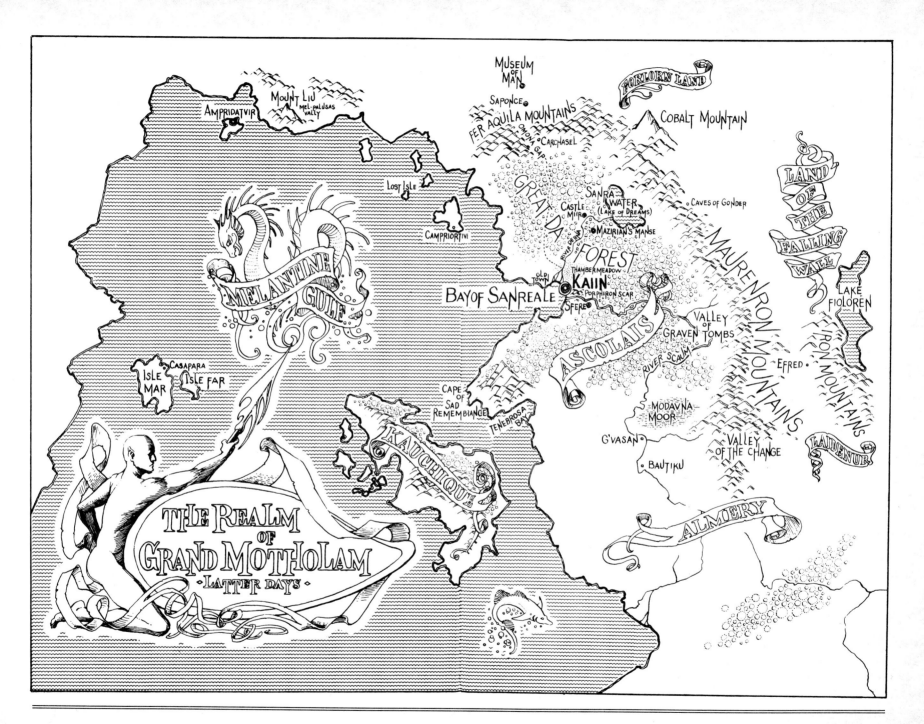

THE REALM OF GRAND MOTHOLAM
·LATTER DAYS·

MUSEUM OF MAN

FORLORN LAND

MOUNT LIU
MEL-PALUSAS VALLY

AMPRIDATVIR

SAPONCE

FER AQUILA MOUNTAINS

COBALT MOUNTAIN

OMONA GAP

CARCHASEL

LAND OF THE FALLING WALL

LOST ISLE

GREAT DA

SANRA WATER
(LAKE OF DREAMS)

CASTLE MIIR

CAVES OF GONDER

CAMPRIORTIVI

MAZIRIAN'S MANSE

MELANTINE GULF

FOREST

RIVER DERNA

THAMBER MEADOW

KAIIN

OLD TOWN

BAY OF SANREALE

PORPHIRON SCAR

MAURENRON MOUNTAINS

LAKE FIOLOREN

SFERE

VALLEY OF GRAVEN TOMBS

ASCOLAIS

IRON MOUNTAINS

CASAPARA

ISLE FAR

ISLE MAR

RIVER SCAUM

EFRED

CAPE OF SAD REMEMBRANCE

TENEBROSA BAY

MODAVNA MOOR

LAIDENUR

KAUCHIQUE

G'VASAN

VALLEY OF THE CHANGE

BAUTIKU

ALMERY

165

LANKHMAR IN THE LAND OF NEHWON

Nehwon is the creation of Fritz Leiber (1910–   ). He has two heroes, the giant Fafhrd and the lithe Gray Mouser, two adventurers who travel about Nehwon wenching, drinking, stealing, fighting, and all else expected of the full life. Nehwon is beset, as are most lands of heroic fantasy, with wizards, magicians, and strange beings. What sets Leiber's stories off from most others is a keen sense of humor; most tales of heroes take themselves much too seriously. Fafhrd and the Gray Mouser are almost human in their weaknesses and pettiness.

This map of Lankhmar, the queen city of Nehwon, is by Tim Kirk. It first appeared in *Amra*.

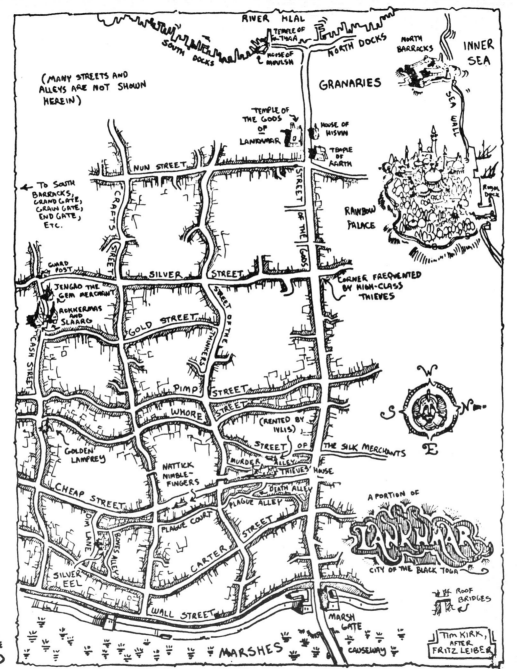

RIVER HLAL

SOUTH DOCKS

TEMPLE OF HA-TH-KA

HOUSE OF MOULSH

NORTH DOCKS

GRANARIES

NORTH BARRACKS

INNER SEA

SEA WALL

(MANY STREETS AND ALLEYS ARE NOT SHOWN HEREIN)

TEMPLE OF THE GODS OF LANKHMAR

HOUSE OF HISVIN

TEMPLE OF AARTH

NUN STREET

TO SOUTH BARRACKS, GRAND GATE, GRAIN GATE, END GATE, ETC.

CRAFTS STREET

STREET OF THE GODS

RAINBOW PALACE

RIVER DOCKS

GUARD POST

SILVER STREET

CORNER FREQUENTED BY HIGH-CLASS THIEVES

JENGAO THE GEM MERCHANT

ROKKERMAS AND SLAARG

GOLD STREET

STREET OF THE THINKERS

CASH STREET

PIMP STREET

WHORE STREET

(RENTED BY IVLIS)

GOLDEN LAMPREY

STREET OF THE SILK MERCHANTS

NATTICK NIMBLE-FINGERS

MURDER ALLEY

THIEVES' HOUSE

CHEAP STREET

DEATH ALLEY

PLAGUE ALLEY

A PORTION OF

DIM LANE

BONES ALLEY

PLAGUE COURT

CARTER STREET

LANKHMAR

SILVER EEL

CITY OF THE BLACK TOGA

ROOF BRIDGES

WALL STREET

MARSH GATE

TIM KIRK, AFTER FRITZ LEIBER

4 SQUARES SOUTH: PLAZA OF DARK DELIGHTS, WITH FOUNTAIN OF DARK ABUNDANCE, SHRINE OF THE BLACK VIRGIN, ETC.

MARSHES

CAUSEWAY

PRYDAIN

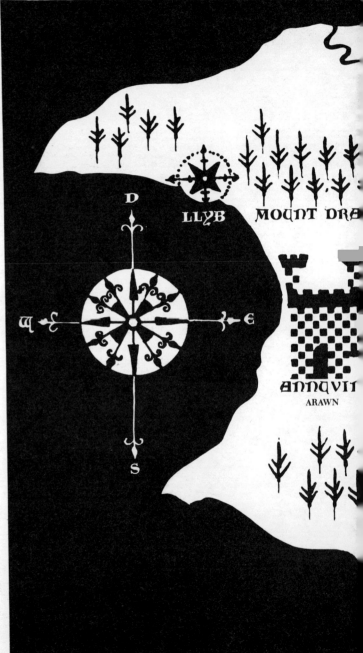

Drawn by Evaline Ness, the maps of Prydain adorn the endpapers of Lloyd Alexander's stories dealing with this mystic realm, published by Holt, Rinehart & Winston from 1964 to 1968. Many fantasy lands are timeless stages where heroes do mighty works. Other fantasy lands have a well-developed history, but are only mapped for one period. Prydain's maps, on the other hand, show a temporal evolution; each of the five novels in the cycle has a different map accompanying it.

The world of Prydain has the flavor of medieval Wales, and the story of the rise and fall of its dynasties and cities reads as real history.

The Book of Three

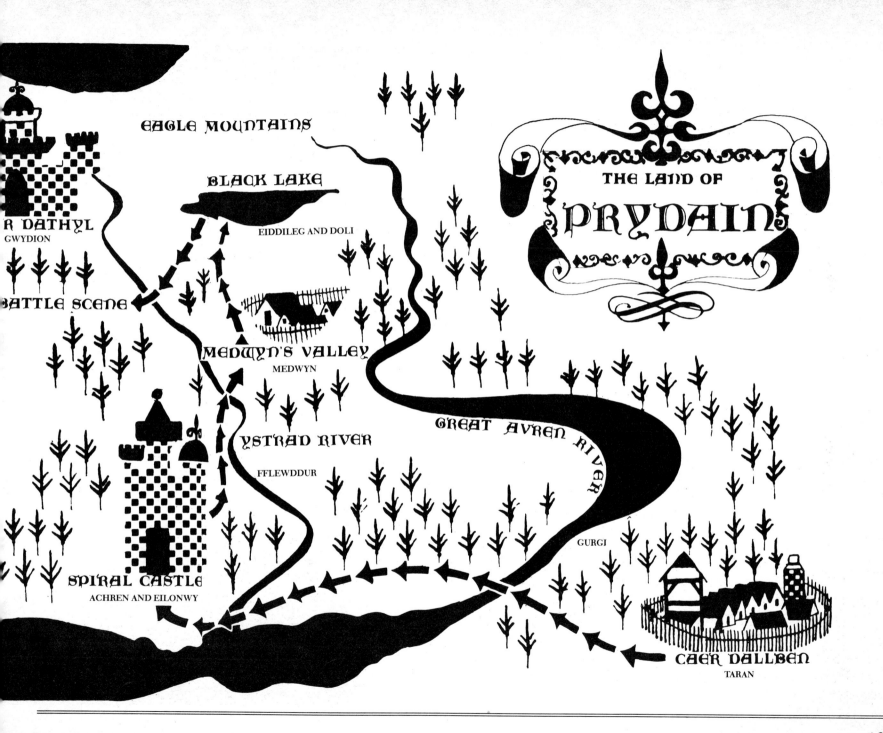

THE LAND OF
PRYDAIN

EAGLE MOUNTAINS

BLACK LAKE

R DATHYL
GWYDION

EIDDILEG AND DOLI

BATTLE SCENE

MEDWYN'S VALLEY
MEDWYN

YSTRAD RIVER

FFLEWDDUR

GREAT AVREN RIVER

GURGI

SPIRAL CASTLE
ACHREN AND EILONWY

CAER DALLBEN
TARAN

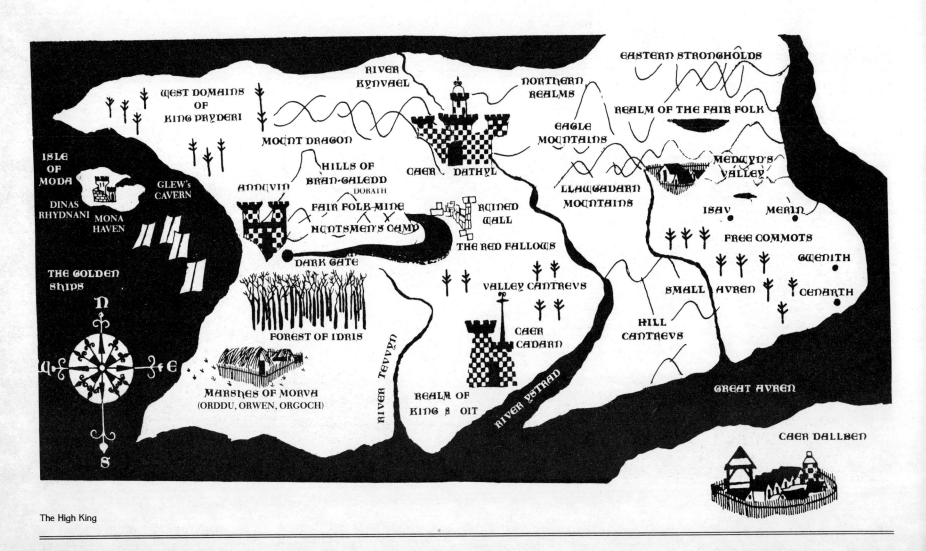

EASTERN STRONGHOLDS

RIVER KYNVAEL

WEST DOMAINS OF KING PRYDERI

NORTHERN REALMS

REALM OF THE FAIR FOLK

MOUNT DRAGON

EAGLE MOUNTAINS

ISLE OF MONA

GLEW's CAVERN

HILLS OF BRAN-GALEDD

DORATH

CAER DATHYL

MEDWYN'S VALLEY

DINAS RHYDNANT

MONA HAVEN

ANNUVIN

FAIR FOLK MINE

LLAWGADARN MOUNTAINS

ISAV

MERIN

HUNTSMEN'S CAMP

THE GOLDEN SHIPS

RUINED WALL

THE RED FALLOWS

FREE COMMOTS

DARK GATE

GWENITH

VALLEY CANTREVS

SMALL AVREN

CENARTH

FOREST OF IDRIS

CAER CADARN

HILL CANTREVS

RIVER TEVVYN

MARSHES OF MORVA
(ORDDU, ORWEN, ORGOCH)

REALM OF KING 8 OIT

RIVER YSTRAD

GREAT AVREN

CAER DALLBEN

The High King

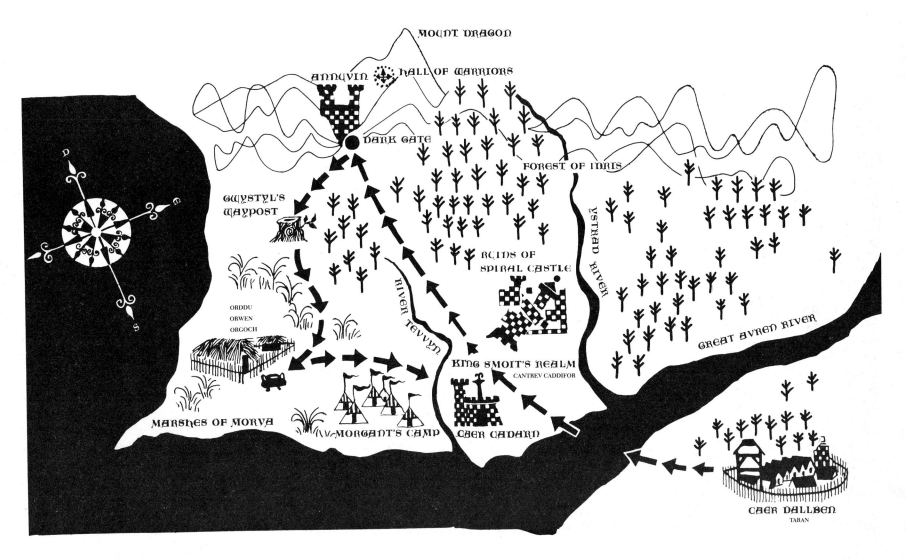

MOUNT DRAGON

ANNUVIN · HALL OF WARRIORS

DARK GATE

GWYSTYL'S WAYPOST

FOREST OF IDRIS

YSTRAD RIVER

RIVER TEVVYN

RUINS OF SPIRAL CASTLE

ORDDU
ORWEN
ORGOCH

GREAT AVREN RIVER

KING SMOIT'S REALM
CANTREV CADDIFOR

MARSHES OF MORVA

MORGANT'S CAMP

CAER CADARN

CAER DALLBEN
TARAN

The Black Cauldron

LEMURIA

Lin Carter (1930–   ) is not only an inspired editor of, and
mapmaker for, the stories of other folk, but also a creator of his
own fantasy worlds. Mr. Carter is very aware of how to put a world
together, having studied the best of them. He has given talks to
groups on how a writer can construct a fantasy world, make a map
of it, and give that world a history and culture.

    Lemuria is one of the ancient prehuman continents
hypothesized by geologists, which has been commandeered by
cultists for their own nefarious purposes. (For full details see L.
Sprague de Camp's *Lost Continents*.) Mr. Carter uses it as
a stage for Thongor and friends to battle pirates, evil druids, and
dragon magicians.

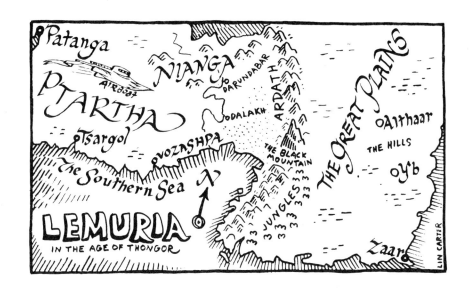

LEMURIA IN THE AGE OF THONGOR

Patanga · NIANGA · PTARTHA · to DARUNDABAR · ODALAKH · ARDATH · Tsargol · OVOZASHPA · The Southern Sea · THE BLACK MOUNTAIN · JUNGLES · THE GREAT PLAINS · Althaar · THE HILLS · Oyb · Zaar

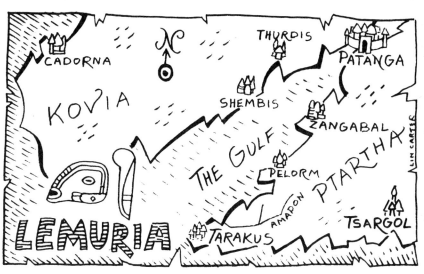

LEMURIA

CADORNA · KOVIA · THURDIS · PATANGA · SHEMBIS · THE GULF · ZANGABAL · PELORM · AMADON · PTARTHA · TARAKUS · Tsargol

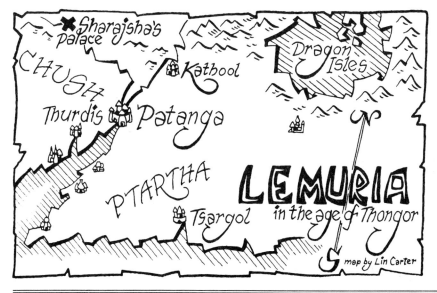

LEMURIA in the age of Thongor

Sharajsha's palace · CHUSH · Kathool · Dragon Isles · Thurdis · Patanga · PTARTHA · Tsargol · map by Lin Carter

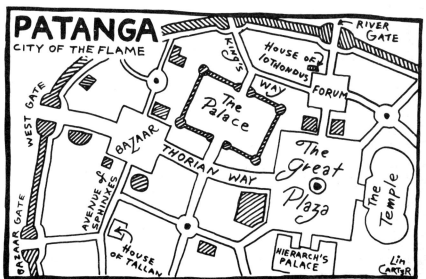

PATANGA
CITY OF THE FLAME

RIVER GATE · King's · HOUSE OF IOTHONDUS · FORUM · WEST GATE · WAY · The Palace · BAZAAR · The Great Plaza · THORIAN WAY · The Temple · BAZAAR GATE · AVENUE of SPHINXES · HOUSE OF TALLAN · HIERARCH'S PALACE

MARS

In the late 1940s Dell published specialized *genre* literature in the categories of Romance, Westerns, Adventure, and Mysteries. For some strange reason science fiction was published under the Mystery imprint. One of the really fine collections of stories was *Invasion from Mars: interplanetary stories* (New York: Dell, 1949) selected by Orson Welles. It included the script for the famous Welles' broadcast among its ten stories. The back cover map reproduced here illustrated Ray Bradbury's "The Million Year Picnic," a story of a colony of scientists trapped on Mars after Earth is destroyed by war. The phrase "Martians Seen Here" refers to the Earth family seeing their reflection in a canal, and realizing that they must build a new world.

THE SEVERN VALLEY AT BRICHESTER

If you get out a map of England, you will find that the Severn River is real, as is Berkeley, Route A.38, and the Cotswolds. J. Ramsey Campbell is a Liverpudlian who started writing stories in a Lovecraftian vein set in Massachusetts and in the Arkham country. They didn't work so he switched the locale to the Severn Valley in Glouchestershire, and succeeded in capturing a vital atmosphere. The Lovecraft *pastiche* always concerns ancient books and magic lore leading to contact with the Old Ones (who at times take on science fictional trappings and become extraterrestrial beings rather than supernatural). Atmosphere is all in these stories.

The arrow pointing to Exham is an "in" joke for readers of H. P. Lovecraft: his story "The Rats in the Walls" is set at Exham Priory.

This map was drawn by Frank Utpatel as the endpaper illustration for Mr. Campbell's *The Inhabitant of the Lake* (Sauk City, Wis.: Arkham House, 1964).

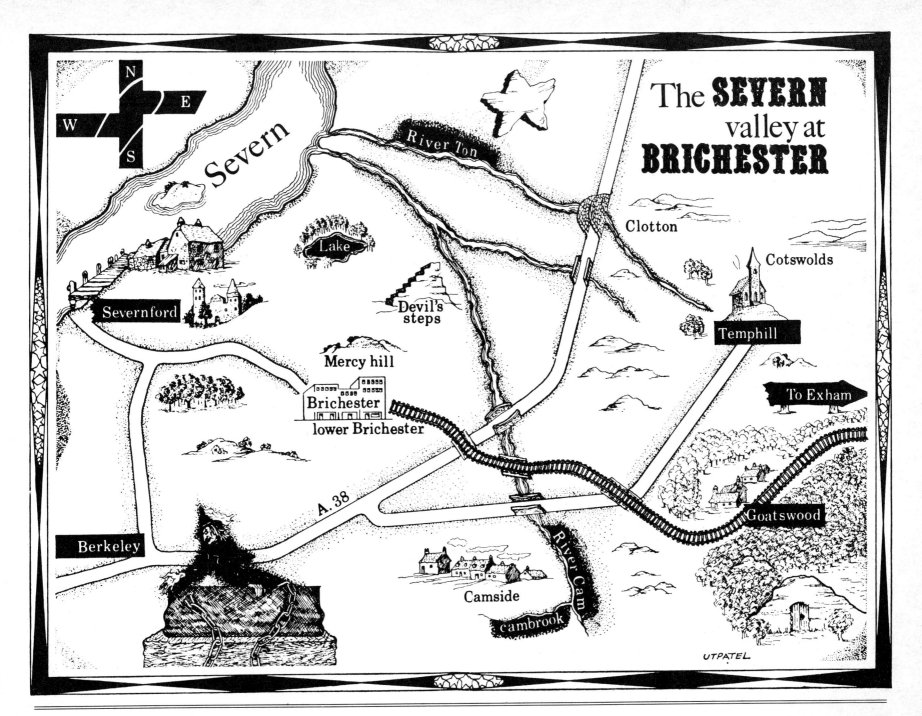

DUNE

Dune (Philadelphia: Chilton, 1965) by Frank Herbert is a huge novel of interplanetary intrigue set mainly upon the desert world of Dune. The map does not do justice to Mr. Herbert's vivid description of human beings surviving in a desolate world where water is the great treasure, but it is an admirable guide for following the action. One item, however, does call for an explanation: the Worm Line refers to the farthest point north to which the gigantic worms infesting Dune will go. Dune is an unpleasant place to live, but does provide interesting reading about its ecology. Part of Frank Herbert's reason for writing it was to interest people in ecology and environmental planning in the years before public attention was peaked.

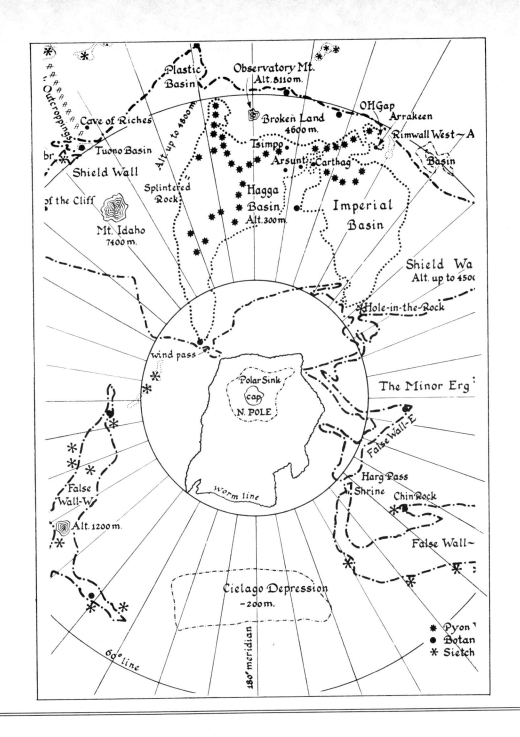

MONGO

First, of course, is Buck Rogers. You never heard the phrase "that crazy Flash Gordon stuff" did you? But if not first, Flash is at least second in personifying the comic book (or strip) science fiction adventure story. Over all, the art work was probably better in Flash Gordon than in Buck Rogers. Flash, Dr. Zarkhov, and Dale Arden journey to Mongo and there encounter Shark Men, Hawk Men, Lion Men, and even Men Men. Ming the Merciless, Kang the Cruel, and a host of lesser villains bedevil Flash and his companions, but in the end Flash wins out. This map is from the back cover of *Flash Gordon,* September 1966, published by King Features Syndicate.

MAP OF THE PLANET MONGO

MONGO IS APPROXIMATELY ONE HALF THE DIAMETER OF EARTH BUT HAS A GRAVITATIONAL DENSITY THAT IS ONLY SLIGHTLY LESS. IT IS A RELATIVELY YOUNG WORLD WITH TOWERING MOUNTAINS NOT YET WORN SMOOTH BY TIME AND MANY AREAS OF VOLCANIC ACTIVITY. ITS VEGETATION IS STILL LIMITED TO ISOLATED AREAS OF BOTANICAL GIANTS. BIOLOGICALLY, IT IS STILL IN THE ERA OF REPTILIAN GIANTS. MAN EVOLVED FAST INTO DIVERSE RACES, MANY OF WHICH POSSESS AMAZINGLY ADVANCED TECHNOLOGY WHILE OTHERS STILL LIVE IN PRIMITIVE AND UNEXPLORED REGIONS.

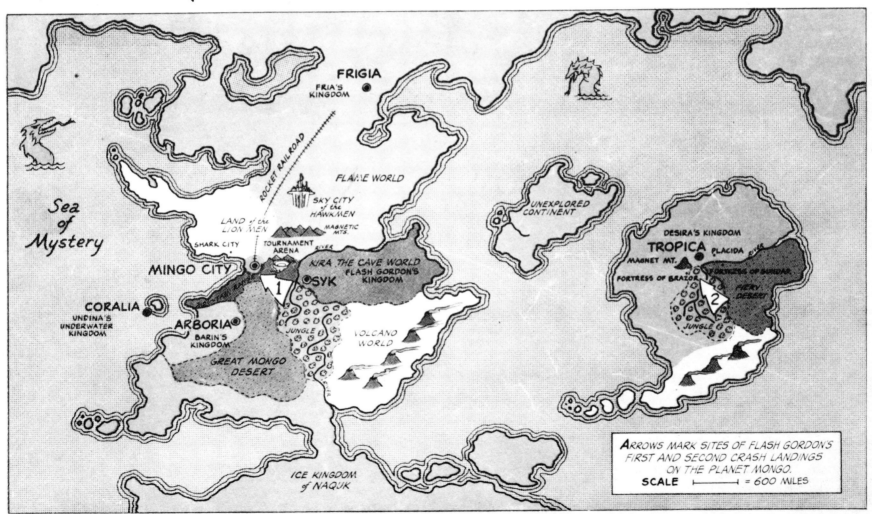

FRIGIA
FRIA'S KINGDOM

Sea of Mystery

FLAME WORLD

ROCKET RAILROAD

SKY CITY of the HAWKMEN

LAND of the LION MEN

MAGNETIC MTS.

SHARK CITY

TOURNAMENT ARENA

RIVER

MINGO CITY

KIRA THE CAVE WORLD
FLASH GORDON'S KINGDOM

1

SYK

CORALIA
UNDINA'S UNDERWATER KINGDOM

ARBORIA
BARIN'S KINGDOM

JUNGLE

VOLCANO WORLD

GREAT MONGO DESERT

RIVER

UNEXPLORED CONTINENT

DESIRA'S KINGDOM
TROPICA
PLACIDA RIVER

MAGNET MT.

FORTRESS OF BRAZOR

FORTRESS OF SUNDAR

FIERY DESERT

2

JUNGLE

ICE KINGDOM of NAQUK

ARROWS MARK SITES OF FLASH GORDON'S FIRST AND SECOND CRASH LANDINGS ON THE PLANET MONGO.
SCALE ⊢————⊣ = 600 MILES

ATLANTIS

This map is, of course, a fraud. Atlantis as described by Plato is quite different in layout, and Plato is the first word on Atlantis. The best study of the entire Atlantis myth is L. Sprague de Camp's *Lost Continents: the Atlantis theme in history, science, and literature* (New York: Dover, 1970). The Atlantis shown here is based on the stories by Henry Kuttner dealing with the adventures of Elak, exiled prince of Cyrene, and is drawn by Jack Gaughan. It appeared in *Fantastic Swordsmen* (New York: Pyramid, 1967).

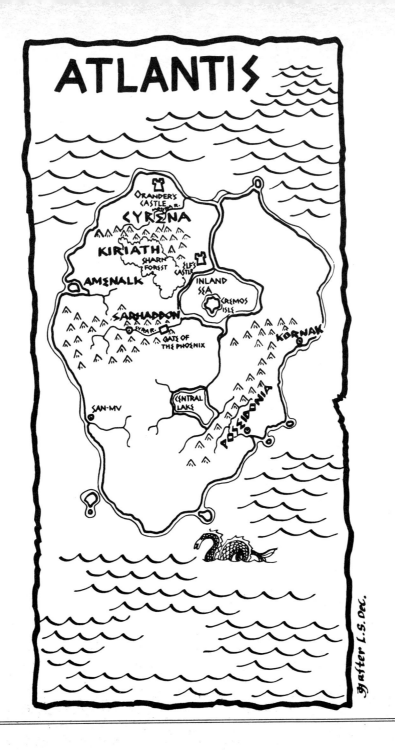

TYROS

John Jakes (1932–   ) writes in the vein of heroic fantasy. His
hero, Brak, is a timeless fellow on his way from his home in the
north to a more southerly realm. Along the way he finds
adventures, monsters, and maidens needing rescue. There is some
temporal development but not very much, so the series is
essentially a "cookie cutter" one; the episodes are virtually
interchangeable. The stories are imaginative, but they are quite
derivative from the Conan stories by Robert E. Howard. The world
of Conan seems real, the ancient cities feel like ancient cities, the
monsters appear to have been waiting for a victim for a thousand
years, the magicians have studied an ancient lore; but the stories by
Jakes too often seem to have cardboard props for cities, and
monsters patched together ten minutes before the hero destroys
them. The map by Jack Gaughan is from *Fantastic Swordsmen*
(New York: Pyramid, 1967).

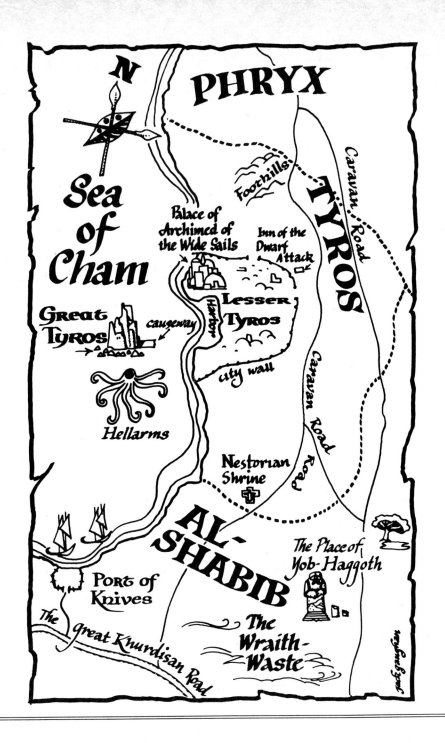

KANTHOS, SULMANNON, AND ANZOR

This map was drawn by Alex Dain to show the areas of action in his book *Bane of Kanthos* (New York: Ace Books, 1969). Mr. Dain submitted this map with his manuscript to his publisher. Most publishers have a house artist draw any maps they use, and as we saw earlier, sometimes this can lead to errors. In many cases the publisher unfortunately decides not to include a map, and the reader is left to figure out for himself the geography of the story.

GWYNEDD AND ITS NEIGHBORS

Medieval Wales has been an inspiration for many writers of fantasy. Lloyd Alexander's world of Prydain has a Welsh flavor, and Evangeline Walton draws directly from Welsh mythology. Various editions of *The Mabinogian* are a ready source of lore. Katherine Kurtz, however, creates a world that is both very Welsh and very much her own. It might be a parallel world in another time, but there are differences. . . .

A world church of Christian appearances spiritually dominates the known world (though there are Moors mentioned), and is engaged in a campaign against the Deryni. The Deryni are a remnant of an older group of psychically endowed people who had dominated Gwynedd for generations until their cruel reign was overthrown. There is a natural fear and suspicion of those left, though a few have risen high in the service of the normal human monarchs. The Church accuses them of witchcraft and dealings with the Devil if they use their psychic powers. As the stories unfold, it seems many, if not all, people have latent psychic powers and the Deryni then appear as not so terribly alien, but more as people with gifted talents in the use of their mind powers.

Against this background, Katherine Kurtz has written a series of novels rich in court intrigue and in colorful battle scenes. *Camber of Culdi* and *Saint Camber* give the historic background of the Deryni domination and of its overthrow, while *Deryni Rising, Deryni Checkmate,* and *High Deryni* (all published by Ballantine Books) tell the story of King Kelson of Gwynedd and Duke Alaric Morgan, his trusted Deryni advisor, attempting to survive all the hazards of their enemies.

PERN

Many science fiction writers have told tales about human colonization of other worlds, and of backwater worlds reverting to primitive conditions when cut off from communication with Earth. Pern, created by Anne McCaffrey, is in the Sagittarian Sector, one world of several circling a G-type star. The colonists discover to their sorrow that dangerous "Threads," a monstrous life form from another world, periodically invades Pern. Pern's technology is destroyed, but the inhabitants manage to breed a "dragon" race linked telepathically to certain human beings and it is able to fight the invader. Between passes of the Red Star (as the world of the Threads was called) humankind prospered. In the series "The Dragonriders of Pern," currently in three volumes published by Ballantine Books, Anne McCaffrey chronicles battles with the Threads as well as the decline and revitalization of the Dragonriders. Weyrs are dragon-nests and Holds are underground settlements to which the Pernese flee when endangered.

This map of Pern was drawn by Bob Porter.

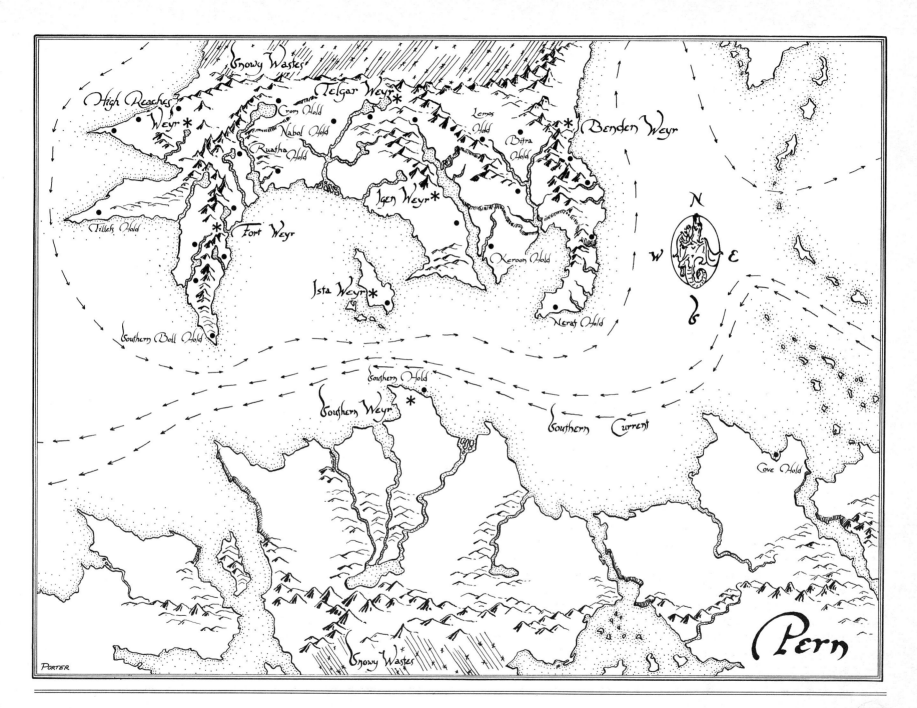

Pern

THE DUCHY OF STRACKENZ

Harry Paget Flashman is roguish and ofttimes villainous, but never a real villain—at least in his own eyes. George MacDonald Fraser, tireless editor of the "Flashman Papers," is giving us the adventures of Flashie (as his friends call him) on the installment plan. Flashman has the knack of being on the losing side in most of the armed conflicts of the nineteenth century, but he always comes away covered with glory. He cheats, lies, steals, cuckolds, betrays—the Compleat Swine. In *Royal Flash* (New York: Alfred A. Knopf, 1970), from which this map is taken, Flashie becomes embroiled in the Schleswig-Holstein Affair, engaging in Zendanian adventures as the double of the Duke of Strackenz.

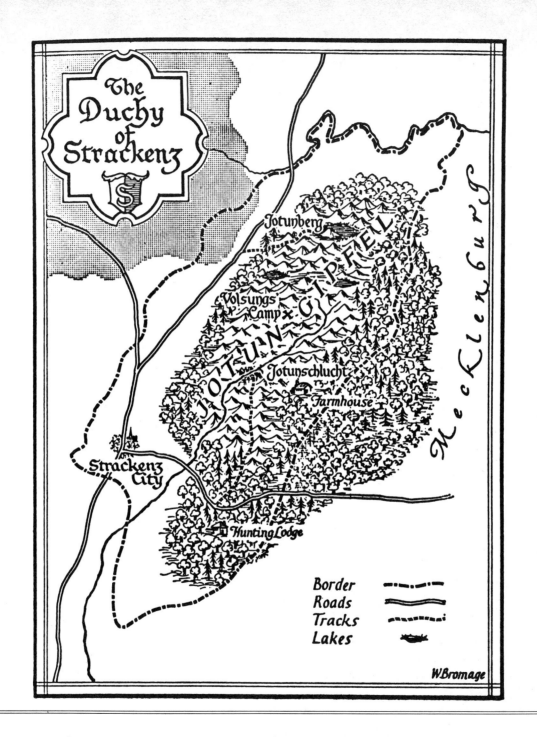

THE WORLDS OF H. P. LOVECRAFT

The literary fortunes of H. P. Lovecraft (1890–1937) are again on the rise in the United States. The stories he wrote fall into a few general groups though all are fantasy, usually ghostly (and ghastly). Arkham is a mythical New England town which vaguely corresponds to Salem. It is the scene of frightful doings and trafficking with monstrous Beings from Beyond. Drawing on his own knowledge of New England, Lovecraft creates a convincing countryside, a real background for his surreal monsters. The map reproduced here, by famous cartoonist Gahan Wilson, first appeared in *The Arkham Collector* for Summer 1970. Lovecraft did sketch some maps of Arkham and Innsmouth, another imaginary town, but this is the first real map. It influenced Eric Carlson to draw a map of Innsmouth appearing in *Nyctalops* No. 6.

Lovecraft also wrote another cycle of stories laid in his Dreamland. These stories were heavily influenced by the works of Lord Dunsany. They have an ethereal quality about them that suits the subject. This map by Jack Gaughan was based on the geography of Dreamland worked out by L. Sprague de Camp and reproduced in his *Fantastic Swordsmen* (New York: Pyramid, 1967).

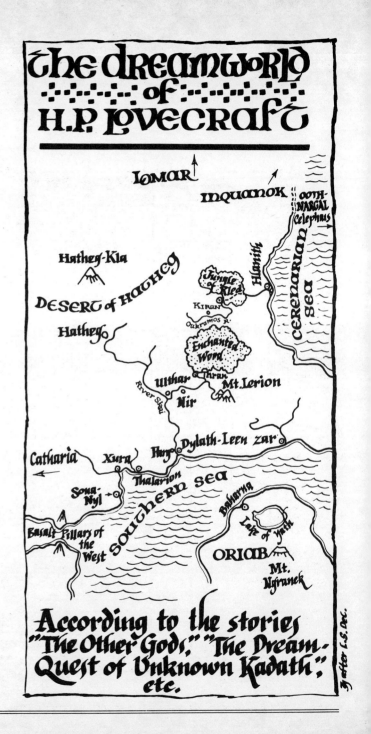

The Dreamworld of H.P. Lovecraft

According to the stories "The Other Gods," "The Dream-Quest of Unknown Kadath," etc.

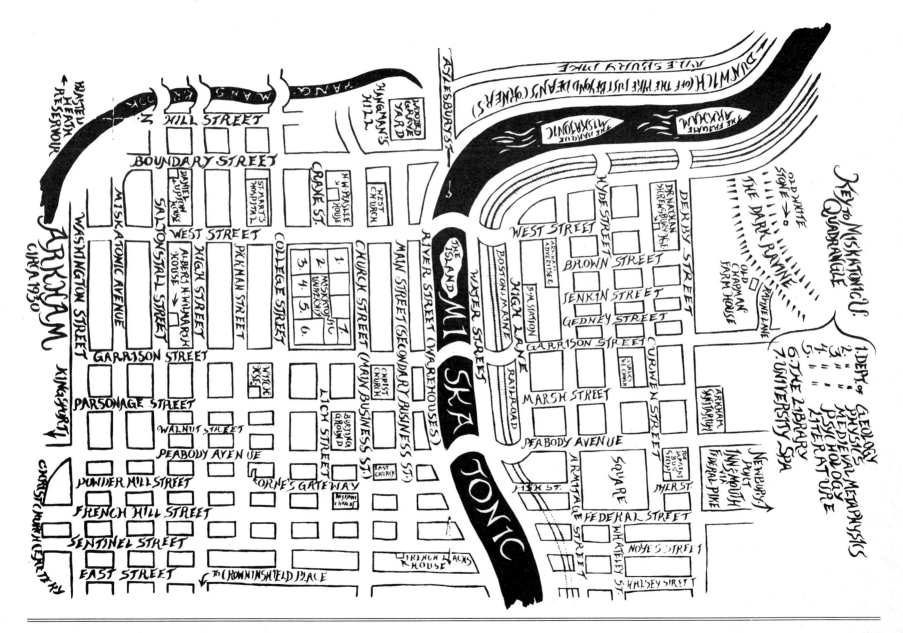

MAFRICA

The term "secondary universe" means a fully realized imaginary
world. For the most part these worlds are literary, if science fiction
and fantasy may be called "literature." A nonliterary secondary
universe type of some size is the war games map. War games and
board games are closely related, the board being a highly stylized
map. In one sense chess is a war game played on a stylized field
with standard pieces. Variations can be introduced in fairy chess
(actually "chesses" since there are so many), but it is in war games
played with miniature figures that the possibilities for maps become
almost infinite. In some versions the players set up the terrain
before each game, creating a unique world. For the war gamers
with limited imagination, Jack Scruby, one of the larger dealers in
military miniatures, has created a series of maps to suggest terrains
for battle. As in actual warfare, Romans and Britons have different
battle rules than Austrians and Prussians in the Seven Years War.
Some terrains are better for chariots than for elephants. One of his
maps is set up for wars of the Napoleonic Era, others for ancient
(Greek and Roman) battles. Mafrica is a jumble of real names and
some imagined ones with a salting of nongeographical actual
names and a few straight descriptive ones such as "The Black
Cliffs." The terrain is varied enough for several different time
periods (not in the same game, though), and offers a wide
stage for action.

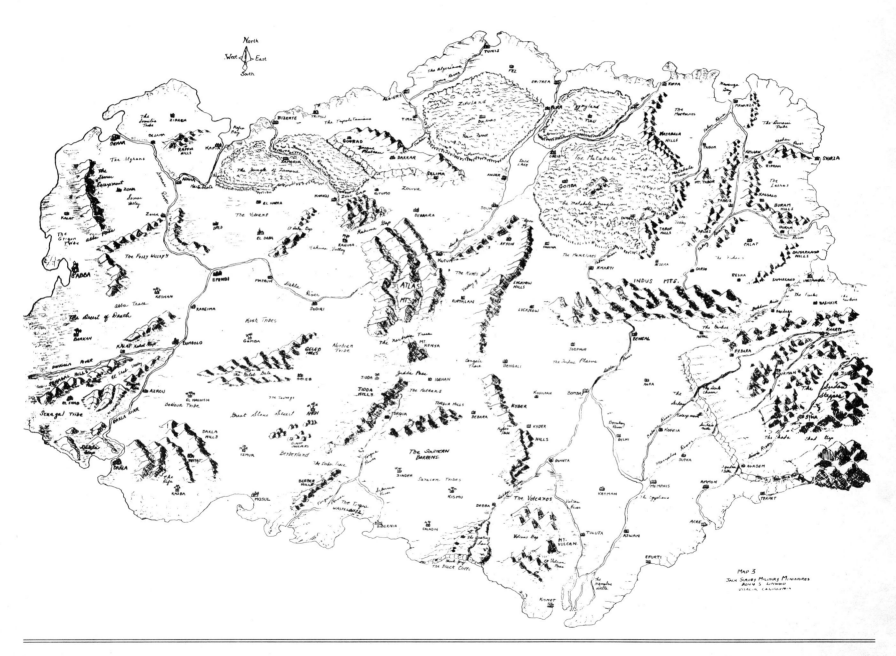

THE
BEKLAN
EMPIRE

Essentially, *Shardik* (New York: Simon & Schuster, 1974) by
Richard Adams (1920–   ) is the story of Kelderek, an Ortelgan
hunter, who rescues a giant bear which he comes to believe is a
manifestation of the Deity. As the prophet militant, Kelderek leads
the Ortelgans to a conquest of the Beklan Empire. At the height of
his power, Kelderek follows Shardik into the wilderness to death
and glory. Almost as an afterthought, we find that Bekla, for all its
splendor, is a rather small part of the world, and that there is a hint
of a powerful empire downstream.

The endpaper map is by Rafael Palacios. Two map illustrations
within the book are by Marilyn Hemmett and show the island of
Quiso and the city of Bekla itself.

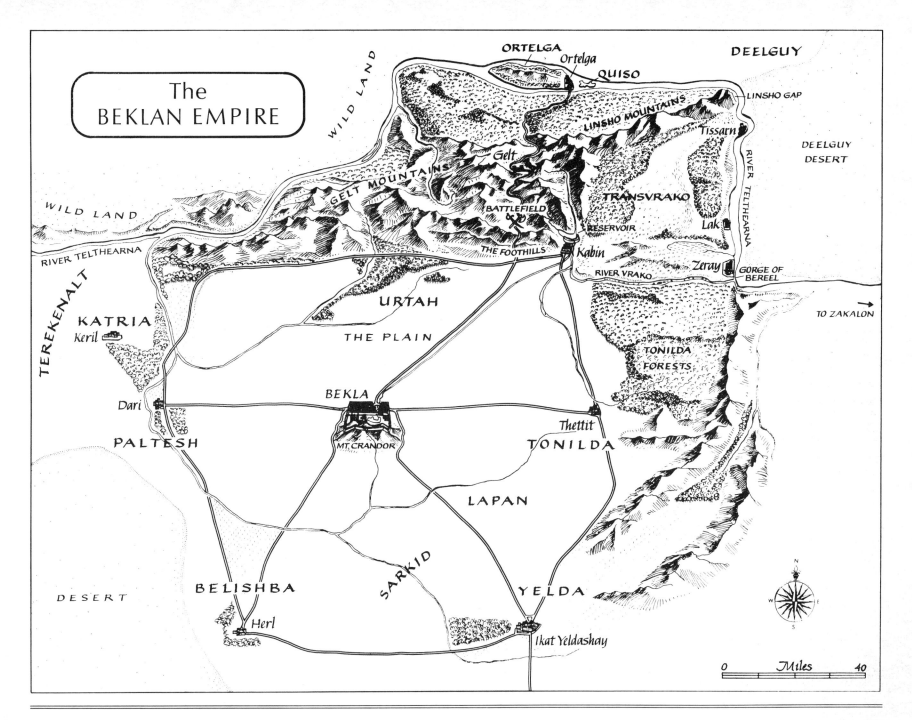

The
BEKLAN EMPIRE

WILD LAND

ORTELGA
Ortelga

DEELGUY

QUISO

LINSHO GAP

LINSHO MOUNTAINS

Tissarn

DEELGUY
DESERT

GELT MOUNTAINS

Gelt

TRANSVRAKO

BATTLEFIELD

RESERVOIR

Lak

RIVER TELTHEARNA

WILD LAND

THE FOOTHILLS

Kabin

RIVER TELTHEARNA

ZERAY

GORGE OF
BEREEL

RIVER VRAKO

TEREKENALT

URTAH

TO ZAKALON

KATRIA

Keril

THE PLAIN

TONILDA
FORESTS

Dari

BEKLA

Thettit

PALTESH

MT. CRANDOR

TONILDA

LAPAN

DESERT

BELISHBA

SARKID

YELDA

Herl

Ikat Yeldashay

N

0   Miles   40

MAP OF
FLORIN AND
GUILDER

As the purported abridger of *The Princess Bride: S. Morgenstern's Classic Tale of True Love and High Adventure, the "good parts" version*, William Goldman displays a sense of humor that is droll and puckish. Goldman, author of such novels as *Soldier in the Rain* and *Boys and Girls Together*, and script writer for the movie "Butch Cassidy and the Sundance Kid," tells us of his early childhood encounter with this *(The Princess Bride)* classic story. Years later he finds that his father had only read him the "good parts" and now Goldman performs that service for the rest of us.

The highly decorative map by Lowell Hess was not included in the Harcourt Brace Jovanovich edition. But it definitely is in the Ballantine paperback edition. The story is about Buttercup, the most beautiful girl in the world; Westley, a farm hand who makes good (sort of); Prince Humperdink; and other interesting folk. It's silly to try to abridge an abridgement, so I really urge everyone to read this funny story.

THE WORLDS OF ERIC JOHN STARK

Eric John Stark was born of Earth parents on the planet Mercury. After their death, he was raised (a là Tarzan) as N'Chaka by Mercurian aborigines until "rescued" by Simon Ashton, a colonial official. Stark travels to many worlds, often operating beyond the law: he visits the gaseous Red Sea of Venus, he roves the desert world of Mars, he travels beyond the solar system. Skaith is a dying backwater planet in the Orion Spur, a single spaceport serving the entire planet. Simon Ashton vanishes while investigating conditions there, and Stark follows in an attempt to save his foster parent. Skaith is governed by a warrior class called Wandsmen who, to retain their power, forbid emigration and rigidly control off-world trade. Stark destroys their power, allying himself with groups discontented with the rule of the Wandsmen. These three maps show Stark's travels on Skaith as chronicled by Leigh Brackett in *The Ginger Star* (New York: Ballantine, 1974), *The Hounds of Skaith* (New York: Ballantine, 1974), and *The Reavers of Skaith* (New York: Ballantine, 1976). Not only does he challenge the Wandsmen, he controls their wild telepathic hounds and bests interplanetary pirates who attempt to loot Skaith.

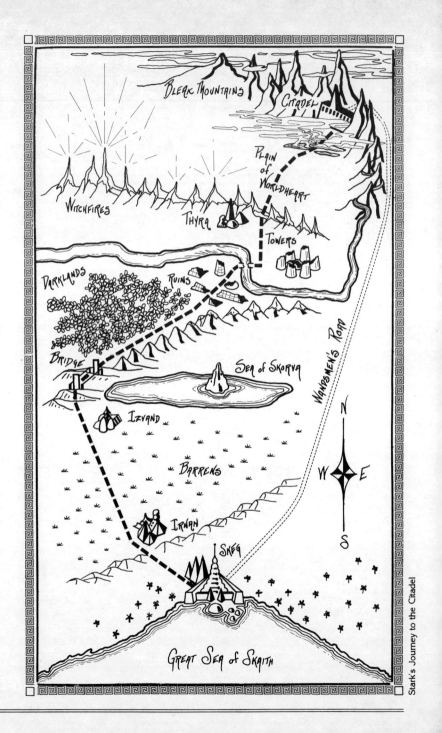

Stark's Journey to the Citadel

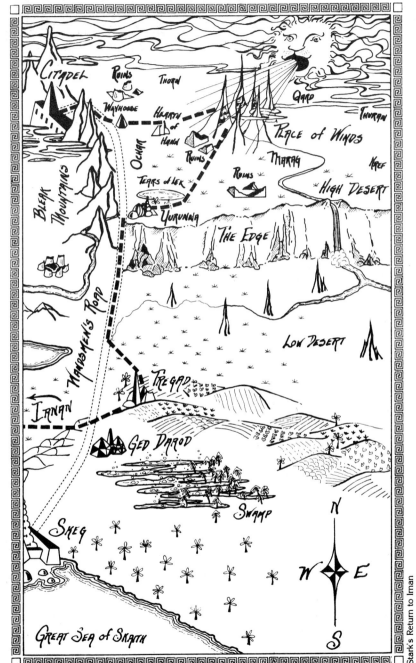

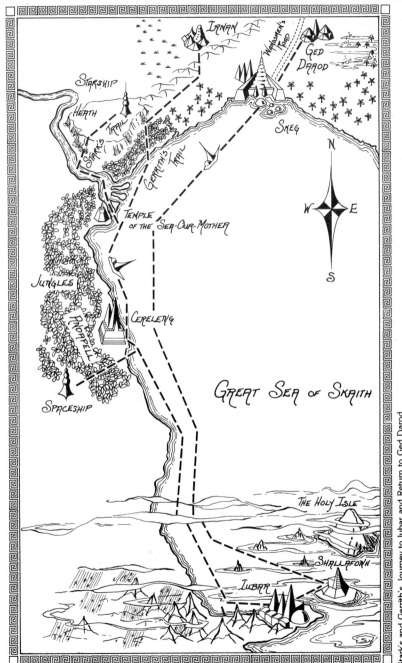

203

THE FOUR LANDS

This map for *The Sword of Shannara* (New York: Ballantine/Del Rey Books, 1977) by Terry Brooks was redrawn by the Brothers Hildebrandt from a sketch by the author.

While never stated, there are strong hints that this is supposed to be our own world after nuclear wars. Mankind develops offshoots which are given names from mythology (Druids, Dwarfs, etc.). The Elves seem to be something else, perhaps extraterrestrials, perhaps an ancient Earth race. Maybe in future works set in this world we will have the answer. Shea Ohmsford is half-human and half-Elf in ancestry, being the last heir to the Elvin throne, and the only being able to wield the mythic Sword of Shannara against the Warlock Lord. The Sword has the interesting property of revealing the Truth, something the Warlock dares not face.

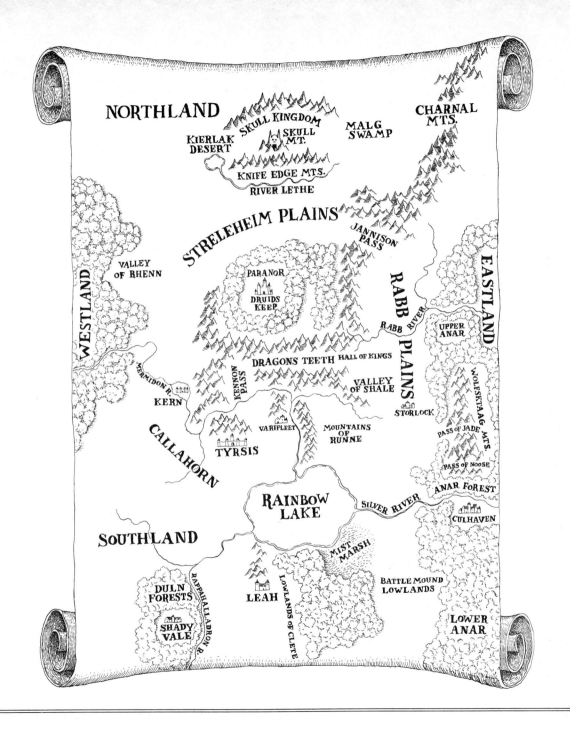

THE LAND

This map of The Land by Lynn K. Plagge appears in each of the three volumes of "The Chronicles of Thomas Covenant the Unbeliever" *(Lord Foul's Bane, The Illearth War,* and *The Power That Preserves)* (New York: Ballantine Books, 1978) by Stephen R. Donaldson.

Thomas Covenant, a leper, is snatched three times (actually four, but one does not count) from this world to the world of The Land where he is considered the promised savior to challenge Lord Foul, The Land's version of Satan. It takes three volumes finally to lay Foul low and bring an age of healing to The Land; three volumes in which Covenant brings grief as well as salvation to those who believe in him. Donaldson's portrayal of Covenant and the spiritual rot that afflicts his soul while leprosy afflicts his body overwhelms the fantasy elements of the first volume. But by the third volume, Covenant accepts his lot as savior. When the epic is ended, we have had a world created for us, from the healing mud, Hurtloam, to the citadel of evil, Foul's Creche.

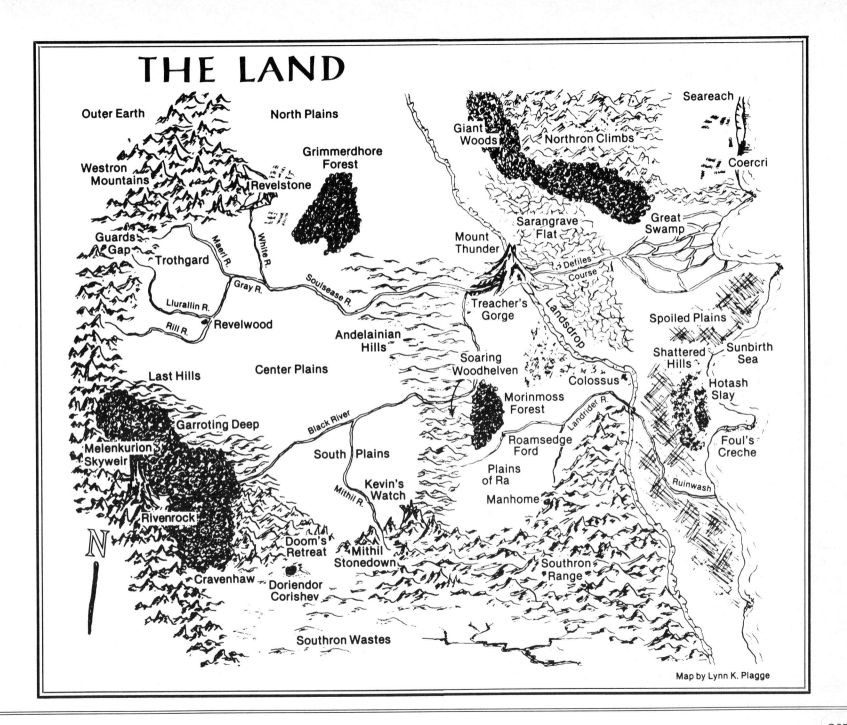

THE LAND

Outer Earth

North Plains

Westron Mountains

Revelstone

Grimmerdhore Forest

Guards Gap

Trothgard

Maeril R.

White R.

Gray R.

Llurallin R.

Rill R.

Revelwood

Soulsease R.

Andelainian Hills

Center Plains

Last Hills

Garroting Deep

Black River

Melenkurion Skyweir

South Plains

Rivenrock

Mithil R.

Kevin's Watch

Doom's Retreat

Mithil Stonedown

Cravenhaw

Doriendor Corishev

Southron Wastes

Giant Woods

Northron Climbs

Seareach

Coercri

Sarangrave Flat

Mount Thunder

Defiles

Course

Landsdrop

Treacher's Gorge

Soaring Woodhelven

Colossus

Morinmoss Forest

Roamsedge Ford

Plains of Ra

Manhome

Landrider R.

Spoiled Plains

Shattered Hills

Sunbirth Sea

Hotash Slay

Foul's Creche

Ruinwash

Southron Range

N

Map by Lynn K. Plagge

Afterword

The foregoing pages have been offered with a variety of purposes in mind. If the reader has been entertained, the compiler will feel justified in his labors. If the reader has been intrigued by the whole field of cartographic fantasy and seeks to pursue it beyond the scope of this brief prolegomenon, the compiler will be happy. If the reader is inspired to draw maps of hitherto unmapped lands of imagination, the compiler will be overjoyed. Maps of imaginary lands will be with us as long as mankind has imagination. It is to be hoped that *An Atlas of Fantasy* is only a beginning in systematically bringing cartographic fantasy to the public's attention.

Index of Artists

Listed here are all of the artists (when known) whose work is represented in *An Atlas of Fantasy,* followed by the page numbers on which their maps appear.

About the Author

Born November 17, 1937, in Rochester, New York, J. B. Post has always been an avid reader of fantasy and science fiction. As a teenager he cofounded Universe Unlimited, a library-affiliated science fiction group. While working his way through the University of Rochester as a book shelver at the Rochester Public Library, he decided to become a librarian. He received his M.S. from Columbia University's School of Library Service in 1961, and in 1965 he was appointed map librarian of the Free Library in Philadelphia, a position he has held ever since.

As well as being active in the Philadelphia Science Fiction Society, he participates in library and map organizations. He recently edited an issue of the *Drexel Library Quarterly* devoted to map librarianship, and he has written the introduction to the Dover reprint of Nordenskiold's *Facsimile-Atlas.* He is a recognized authority on bibliography, maps, and science fiction, reviewing for such publications as *Library Journal, RQ, The Private Library, Luna,* and the Special Libraries Association Geography and Map Division *Bulletin.*

Mr. Post presently resides in West Philadelphia, with his wife Joyce (also a librarian/author), his young son Jonathan, one Siamese cat, and a book collection.